A Family in Skye
1908-1916

Isobel Macdonald

Foreword by Derek Cooper

Published in Scotland in 1980 by Acair Limited, Cromwell Street Quay, Stornoway, Isle of Lewis.

ISBN 0 86152 055 6

Designed by Mackay Design Associates Limited.
Printed by Nevisprint Limited, Fort William, Scotland.

Contents

Foreword

I write these words of welcome, a birthday greeting for *A Family in Skye*, with great pleasure.

It was in October 1977 that I first saw the manuscript. On my way to catch the *Hebrides* to the Outer Isles, I called at the library in Portree to change my books. As I was leaving Barbara Gillies, the librarian, reached behind her and passed me a typewritten manuscript in a sky-blue cover.

'You might be interested in this,' she said. 'It's all about Portree before the first World War.' I began to read the manuscript on the crossing from Uig to Tarbert. I was halfway through it by the time I left Stornoway on the *Suilven* for Ullapool and I finished it the following night at the Overscaig Hotel on Loch Shin. It was a remarkable book; a unique and engrossing record of a way of life which my generation had only heard about at secondhand. In these typed pages the Edwardian world of Skye came vividly alive. Weaving her own recollections with letters written by her mother, Isobel Macdonald had conjured up life in the lamplit Bank House in Portree with such clarity that you could almost see the coals flaring in the library fire, hear the voices in the nursery and the footsteps on the stairs.

It was a privileged childhood; comparative comfort amid poverty and distress. But seventy years ago it was not considered unusual that the fruits of capital and labour should be distributed with so immoral an imbalance — profligate incomes for the few, hunger and hardship for those who hadn't been able to push their snouts into the bulging trough of Victorian industrial prosperity.

There were maids in the Bank House, social visits to castles and cruises in private yachts; but the children's roots were both peasant and middle class. Although her mother's family were prosperous Paisley merchants, Isobel's father was raised on a hungry croft in Skye, and these two ambivalent threads are woven through the story. Acting out a common paradox of the time, young Ronald Macdonald, whose own father had been evicted ruthlessly from his croft, was assimilated painlessly into the ranks of the professional classes. In due course, he became Lord Macdonald's factor; the crofter's son became the laird's agent and thus was the status quo preserved.

Elizabeth Macdonald had attended Glasgow University to study under A. C. Bradley, the Shakespearean scholar, and her letters are both literate and lively. She had a skill with words, an ability to evoke places and scenes, which her daughter has inherited.

It is, as I write this, exactly two years to the day since I first turned the pages of Isobel's book, and looking through it again, I still find myself entranced by these sharply defined views from the past. It's rather like picking up one of those early stereoscopes and inserting the sepia slides. Gently you bring them into focus and the figures appear in three-dimensional reality. In this book they move as well. There's laughter and joy but pain as well in a world where teeth were pulled and tonsils were extracted without anæsthetic and typhoid would sweep over the island softly like malignant rain. It was an age when death came suddenly and unexpectedly; young mothers succumbed to puerperal fever, children were snuffed out by the handful in uncontrollable epidemics and tuberculosis sat down at every table.

The 1914-18 war came, as Isobel recalls, 'after a summer of sunshine and tranquility'. May 1915 brought short, terrible telegrams to many homes on the island, including the Bank House. Wounded at Festubert, Isobel's father died in 1916 and the family, taken south, did not return to Portree.

'The bitterest part of my grief,' Isobel writes, 'was that I had not said goodbye to all the places by the sea or by the streams and woods that I loved as if they were people. I wanted to put my arms round every tree and kiss every rock before I left them'.

Here, at last, is that long-delayed goodbye, a warm and affectionate farewell to childhood and to Skye. A moving book, and one which will endure.

Derek Cooper
Portree, Isle of Skye
October 1979

Isobel Hay Macdonald, the author, aged 10 years.

Background

This book has been composed around a number of letters written from Portree, Isle of Skye, by Elizabeth Blair Macdonald between 1908 and 1916. Her maiden name was Elizabeth Blair Coats, and she was born at Hayfield, Castlehead, Paisley on April 7th 1870. Her father, Allan Coats, had married Isabella Hay as his second wife (her surname suggested the punning name of their house) and Elizabeth was the second child of this new family. The Coatses of Paisley are descended from a Renfrewshire farmer, George Coats, who towards the end of the eighteenth century married an Englishwoman, Catherine Heywood. Their two sons, Jervis and James, became weavers, but in 1812 Jervis found that defective eyesight made it difficult for him to continue in this craft, which was the town's main occupation, so, as his English mother had brought over the Border a flavoursome recipe for home-cured hams, he started a small grocery business. His sliced ham became so popular that his son William and his grandson Allan established the ham-curing firm of W. and A. Coats, which flourished towards the end of the century. But this modest middle-class prosperity was over-shadowed by the magnificence of James's descendants. He had concentrated on spinning thread, and during the nineteenth century his business expanded into the great Ferguslie mills and the firm of J. and P. Coats, a name still to be found in every workbasket. I have heard that grand-father Allan Coats when attending a Baptist conference in London was asked in awed tones, 'I suppose you are one of the great Paisley Coats family?' 'No,' he replied with a twinkle, 'we are the petty Coats.'

By his first wife he had three children, Jeanie, William and Mary. Mary was a brisk practical warm-hearted girl who took up nursing when Arthur, the youngest child of the second family, her especial care from babyhood and everyone's darling, died of diphtheria at the age of twelve. As he seemed somewhat better he was encouraged to sit up and eat his dinner: almost immediately he collapsed and died, and Mary realised too late that his family's ignorance of elementary nursing had killed him. She trained at the Victoria Infirmary, Glasgow, and spent several years as district-nurse at Tarbert, Loch Fyne, among the herring-fishers, a post which she enjoyed enormously for the scope it gave to her warm humanity, her independent judgement, and her rich sense of humour. It is easy to imagine Aunt Mary moving in the shore-background of *Para Handy*, delivering babies, patching up after festive evenings when the boats were in, and giving good advice or scoldings in broad and pungent Scots. During the period of the letters she was matron of the Victoria Infirmary's convalescent home at Largs. Mother calls her 'wise Mary', and values her advice in times of difficulty.

The eldest of the second family was Allan, the inventor and engineer, an original, quick, affectionate and slightly fanatical man. He invented a more efficient clutch for the early motor-cars, but did not have it patented and commercialised, so it never came to anything. He had a theory about how the heat of the sun reached the earth which was his one subject of conversation for a time; elderly ladies at tea-parties were taken into corners to have the heat of the sun explained to them. He was a dear, but he never made much money, and never married.

Robert who came after mother in the family was a Baptist minister at Handsworth in Birmingham. He married Margaret McConnachie, a charming girl, very gifted artistically and musically. Their daughter Alice Coats, after a career as artist and designer, has become well-known as a horticultural chronicler, author of *Flowers and their Histories*, and *Garden Shrubs and their Histories*, and of *The Quest for Plants*. In 1973 she produced her wonderful record of botanical illustrations, '*The Book of Flowers*'. She died in 1978.

But the person nearest to mother, to whom many of the letters were written, was her sister Agnes, four years younger, a beautiful, intense and rather moody girl. There is a photograph of the two sisters in their twenties; both are somewhat Pre-Raphaelite, but mother, with her blonde hair drawn back from a clear-cut, rounded face above a coral necklace and a wide lace collar looks like the Blessed Damosel, while Agnes with gathered velvet frill, dark cloudy hair and tragic expression reminds one of Rossetti's Prosperine holding the fatal pomegranate. She studied at the Glasgow Art School in the nineties, during its most famous period when the Glasgow school of painters was renowned through Europe; she had a gift for portrait-painting, but not enough determination to break free and find a line for herself. Things were difficult then for a girl without exceptional talent or a private income. She never married, but probably endured the pains of love for some artist met during these years: perhaps for Hamilton Mackenzie who painted her portrait in oils. But finally the vie de Bohème was defeated by family life with its Baptist connection, its Liberal politics and its Temperance enthusiasm. She sank into running the home with her mother and sister Jeanie, but there must have been a sense of frustration and of talents unfulfilled behind her acceptance of such a dull existence. During her mid-thirties her dark waving hair became silver, which made the effect of wide forehead, straight nose and proud sensitive mouth even more striking.

George the youngest son who became an eye-specialist in London was the most brilliant of them all, but I do not remember so much about him as he died in 1915. During the holidays at St Abbs and at Kildonan he was in poor health and I was very young.

Mother was always called Lizzie by her family though she never liked the name. Sometimes her father called her Leezie Lindsay after the girl in the song, 'Will ye gang tae the Hielands, Leezie Lindsay?' She was a very pretty

Elizabeth Blair Macdonald and Agnes Coats.

young woman with soft fair hair, lily and rose colouring and dark blue eyes; a great fascinator and wheedler, so that whenever grandfather was being stern about anything the others would get her to coax him round. She was a gay friendly girl, sparkling with energy, and determined not to waste anything so interesting as her life. First she went to Germany to stay in a pastor's household and learn the language; then she attended A. C. Bradley's English classes at Glasgow University, where her essays and her personality impressed him so much that he presented her with a leather-bound volume of Tennyson's poems as a prize. Qualified in language and literature, she took the only degree open to women at that time, the L.L.A. of St Andrews University, which meant Lady Literate in Arts. Then she turned from the arts to crafts. She was a good cook and had always been interested in household matters, so she went to Miss Black's School of Domestic Management in Glasgow, took the whole course, and gained a diploma which qualified her to teach the subject. Then she applied for a post in Portree, Isle of Skye.

Her parents were dismayed. This lively pursuit of culture and skill had brought her to her mid-twenties, and though there was no harm in a young woman keeping herself busy with such interests, it was time she began to think of marrying and settling down. Suitors had sighed for her, but she had not been specially attracted: all the same, at her age, she should be looking for a husband, not for a post as a cookery-teacher. It was a slight on her father who could well afford to keep her, and if she must gratify this absurd whim of going out to earn, why choose a place in the wild Highlands, a two-day journey by train and boat from her comfortable home? There would be no society there, no concerts, no shops, no eligible men. How would she

9

occupy her time in the evenings? And did she realise how much they would all miss her?

On the afternoon when she was making her last preparations an old friend of the family called. 'Eh, Leezie Lindsay!' she said, 'What's this I hear o' you? You'll gang tae the Hielands and leave us a' oor lanes. Ah weel — may be you'll meet Lord Ronald Macdonald, like the lassie in the sang!' Lizzie laughed, but as she folded her blouses she may have sung it to herself:
'She has kilted her coats o' green satin,
She has kilted them up to the knee;
And she's aff wi' Lord Ronald Macdonald,
His bride and his darling to be.'

Since the Mallaig extension of the West Highland railway was not completed till 1901 she would probably spend a night in Inverness and then travel by the Highland Railway across the desolate Ross-shire moors by Dingwall and Strome Ferry to their newly-opened terminus at Kyle of Lochalsh. Here she would board a small David MacBrayne steamer for the ports of eastern Skye. As often happened, the boat was late in arriving at Portree, and Ronald Macdonald had a long wait. He was one of the younger members of the School Board who had been asked to meet Miss Coats, welcome her to the island, and escort her to her lodgings. At last the scarlet funnel was seen coming round the point and there was a stir of expectancy on the pier. The paddles splashed to a standstill; the boat was tied up; passengers came down the gangway, but for a few moments there was no sign of Miss Coats. Perhaps she felt suddenly nervous, or perhaps — more likely — she had decided to take off the cumbersome hat of the period and gave her soft flaxen hair a touch of the comb before facing her new life. The captain leaned from his little bridge to the tall figure on the pier, 'You will be waiting for the new teacher, Mr. Macdonald. Indeed we are late, and I am sorry for it, but never you mind — she is worth waiting for!'

She had come to the end of her long journey, to an island of the Hebrides, far from home and friends, but she was welcomed with kindness and courtesy beyond what she could have expected. There was a smell of tar, paraffin and salt water in the air: a hill covered with pine trees rose steeply behind the pier, and smoke was drifting from two terraces of grey stone houses. Her box was heaved on to a cart, and she walked to her rooms in the village, escorted by a tall dignified stranger with a soft Highland accent and a prophetic name.

She attacked her work at the school with vigour. Her pupils were gentle, courteous and eager to learn, but as many of them came from croft-houses where the cooking was done on an open fire, sometimes in the middle of the room, she had to simplify Miss Black's methods and start at the very beginning — with weights and measures, and the use of an oven, for instance. She had difficulties with the kitchen range supplied by the authorities, and could not always find the ingredients needed for her lessons. However, as autumn passed into winter she found that Portree had its own social and intellectual activities. Her parents need not have feared that after her work was over she would sit and mope by the light of an oil-lamp in a cam-ceiled room. She was invited out, and there were evenings with the Literary Society where she met Mr. Macdonald again. Perhaps he gave a talk on the historical background of one of Scott's novels: perhaps she recast an essay written for Professor Bradley on *In Memoriam* or the *Idylls of the King*: at any rate, they had the excitement of discovering common intellectual interests. At home Lizzie had called the family kitten Jane Welsh Carlyle, but the others had renamed it, perhaps more appropriately, Spunky. Now at last she met someone who had read Froude's books on the Carlyles; had wrestled with Meredith and Browning and was haunted by the style of Pater. When the summer vacation came she invited her new friend to spend some time in the seaside house rented by her father, to meet her parents and family. Soon afterwards they were engaged, and in 1900 they were married.

Ronald Macdonald was born in 1866 in Glenhinisdale. His father, Peter Macdonald, was a crofter who had been evicted from his croft in Glen Uig by the proprietor, Major William Fraser. This notorious oppressor and rack-renter was an incomer to the island who had sold his estate in the Black Isle of Ross-shire and bought the estates of Kilmuir and Uig from Lord Macdonald, with the hope that by doubling and even trebling the rent of many helpless families in that region of scarcity he might make a better income than he could from the ownership of the richest agricultural land north of the Caledonian Canal. To make their crofts into a farm which he rented to a Mr. Urquhart, a prosperous friend of his who did not belong to Skye and combined farming with keeping the inn at Uig, he evicted a number of crofters and settled them at considerably higher rents in Glenhinisdale, where the land was less good, and where communications with the rest of the world for buying and selling would be very difficult, as the crofts were two miles up a rough track branching from the Uig-Portree road, which in these days would not itself be much of a highway. When Her Majesty's commissioners inquired into the condition of the crofters and cottars of the Highlands and Islands of Scotland in 1884 Peter Macdonald, aged 51, was chosen to voice the grievances of Glenhinisdale, and this is how he described them. One can hear the Highland tone in his speech, and be impressed by his command of English, an acquired tongue to him, spoken infrequently.

'When Major Fraser got the estate our rents were from £5:3/- to £5:10/-, and he raised it to £11 and £13:10/-, except two crofts whose rents were £11, and he raised them to £24:10/- and £25, also an assessment of 2/6d per £1, rendering our condition such that should our rents be reduced to the sum it was before Major Fraser became proprietor, it would take a considerable time before we could clear ourselves of our just debts. Of fifteen crofters our liabilities amount to over £600, and with a few exceptions our credit is gone also, and our stock is unsaleable at this time owing to their impoverished condition. Our houses are scarce habitable, which we cannot repair, owing to our being so poor and to the want of lime and wood. We also suffer great

Elizabeth Blair Coats and Ronald Macdonald in the garden of 'Hayfield', Paisley, where their wedding took place in 1900.

inconvenience from the want of our roads, which were destroyed by the great flood of 1877, and never repaired, though we pay for roads and have done so for a considerable time'.

He tells the commissioners that he has six cows and seven young beasts, two horses, fifty old sheep and twenty hoggs (young sheep). He is paying £24:10/- for his land. The crofters ask that they should get the land in such a way that the proprietor should not raise the rent if they improved their holdings. When asked, 'Would their land bear improvement?' Peter replied, 'Yes, some of them are improvable: the land is bad, but some of it is improvable'. To the question, 'Do you consider the ten acres of arable ground with the produce of your beasts and £16 derived from the sale of beasts is sufficient to keep a family comfortable during the year?' he replied with decision, 'No: it would not keep my family in comfort'.

When the commissioners ask what he would consider a fair rent for his holding, exasperation with Glenhinisdale, to which he had been forced to remove, flashes out, 'I cannot say what would be a reasonable rent for the ugly place. If you ask me what would be a reasonable rent for the place I had before, it was £8 when Major Fraser became proprietor'.

Elsewhere he complains that twenty-five children in Glenhinisdale have had no teaching for the last half-year because there has been no schoolmaster. But during Mr. Alexander Macdonald's interrogation it was shown that considerable effort had been made to get one: the post had been advertised several times, but the only applicant who turned up had been a young lady who asked to be taken to Glenhinisdale in a closed carriage, and as this was not available she left the island. It was the glen's remoteness, not the apathy of the Board, that deprived its children of education.

It must be remembered that Peter Macdonald was emphasising the grievances of all the Glenhinisdale crofters whose spokesman he was, and no doubt he felt strong personal resentment about his eviction from Uig to this isolated place, and about the threefold rise of his rent. £24:10/- was a lot of money to raise annually from the struggling self-contained economy of a crofter. But his land seems to have been well-stocked with beasts, and the fact that it is still owned and managed successfully by his descendants suggests that things were not quite so bad as he made out. On his croft he raised a family of five sons and three daughters; as well as Ronald there were Ewen who became proprietor of Castlebay Hotel in the Isle of Barra, Donald who was a policeman in Glasgow, John who inherited the farm, and Norman who was for a time a store-keeper in South Africa. The daughters were Jessie and Mary who married, and Katie-Ann, also called Catriona, who kept house for her brother John. There must have been very little money available for luxuries like tea and sugar; no doubt they lived on milk, butter and cheese from the cows; fresh or salted mutton from their sheep, with oatcakes and porridge, potatoes and eggs. Grandmother spun yarn from the fleeces, which was woven and made into cloth for the family.

Probably there was a teacher in the glen when Ronald was a boy, for he went on to Portree school and to Glasgow University, where he must have been the traditional poor scholar from the Highlands, living on meagre bursaries with very little help from home. But the strength and clarity of his mind would have been apparent from the first; he read widely, absorbed and meditated ideas, and had a fine sense of proportion. His chief interest was history of which he came to have a large library, and his knowledge of Gaelic, his native language, drew him especially to Highland records and poetry. He took a degree in law; came back to Portree and entered the office of Mr. Alexander Macdonald as a junior assistant.

Alexander Macdonald was one of three sons of Henry Macdonald, an incomer from Dingwall who had married a daughter of Dr. Alex MacLeod who was factor to Lord Macdonald's estates as well as a physician. Henry succeeded his father-in-law as factor, and Alexander succeeded him in 1882; soon his forceful personality became a dominating power in the island. The other sons, Harry and John, made fortunes abroad and came back to Portree as proprietors of fine houses; Harry of Viewfield with its fine portico and tower among woods on the lower slopes of Fingal's Seat, and John of beautiful Redcliffe, standing by the shore in a curve of the bay and looking towards Ben Tianavaig. The commission of 1884 was appointed partly as a result of the Battle of the Braes in 1882. A number of Lord Macdonald's crofter-tenants, enraged by rises in rent and by the loss of free grazing which their fore-fathers had enjoyed on Ben Lee, refused to pay their rents. This was the only means of protest against unfair dealing that the crofters could use, and in this case their determined resistance eventually gave them rights, and ended long years of humiliation and injustice. When the sheriff-officer came to summons them for non-payment they pelted him with stones and clods and forced him to burn the summonses. About ten days later the Sheriff, the Procurator-Fiscal and a posse of fifty policemen from Glasgow marched from Portree to arrest the rebels; they were met by an army of men and women throwing stones and screaming curses, so that they had to charge with batons before they could carry off their prisoners. As the rebellion had occurred on Lord Macdonald's estates, his factor, Mr. Alexander, was interrogated at considerable length by the commissioners. Early in the questioning it appeared that he was factor not only for the Macdonald estates, but for those of Macleod of Macleod, Major Fraser of Kilmuir (who had evicted grandfather), Mr. Macdonald of Skeabost and Mr. Macalister of Strathaird. They decided to look into this. 'The population of Skye, I understand, is from 16,000-17,000' — 'Yes'.

'You hold a number of offices yourself?' — 'Yes, I do'.

'Am I wrong in saying that of the population of 17,000 more than 15,000 are under you in one form or another?' — 'My experience has been that they are above me'.

'Will you kindly mention the offices you hold in Skye?' — 'I am bank agent and solicitor, and I was elected clerk of the Portree school board. I am also distributor of stamps and collector of taxes'.

It appears that he is also captain of volunteers, member of five school boards and collector for roads. One of the Commissioners looked at the confident burly man and asked him:-

'Are you pleased with yourself?' — 'I daresay if I were asked I am not a bit more pleased than the crofters are'.

'Are there many law-agents in Skye?' — 'There are only two at present, and I don't think I make what would keep me in tea at law. I have always discouraged law, and so did my father before me'.

'Don't you think that in a large population of this kind matters should be a little more distributed?' — 'I have not the slightest objection to another agent coming here, and if he makes enough to keep him in tea I will be very surprised'.

Alexander Macdonald was evidently the uncrowned king of the island: the farmers and shop-keepers, as well as the crofters, must have met him at every turn as rent-collector, bank-manager and law-agent. In fact, if Mr. Macdonald took a dislike to you, you would not have a hope in Skye. Yet he was not an unkindly man: the Commissioners do not bring any instances of cruelty or oppression against him. An engraved portrait of Mr. Alexander used to hang above our library mantelpiece: a sturdy man wearing a tweed suit of striking check, with a round cannon-ball head slightly raised as if listening. His eyes were bold and choleric: his moustache bristled. Even when confined in a frame he radiated power and mastery.

The son of the evicted crofter from poor Glenhinisdale became the clerk, the assistant, and eventually the successor of this lord of the isle. Alexander Macdonald died at Edinburgh in 1897, and Ronald Macdonald became manager of the National Bank, factor of the Macdonald estates and heir to the law-business; the fact that he had the same surname as his patron helped him to continue its tradition. Mr. George Fraser joined him in the law-firm of Macdonald and Fraser which continued in Portree under the same name till the end of 1978. The Crofters' Holdings Act of 1886 fixed rents and gave security of tenure: Ronald Macdonald worked with the Commission and with the Congested Districts Board to carry out its recommendations. He was always interested in crofters' affairs, and was consulted by Lord Pentland, Secretary for Scotland and responsible for much of the legislation in the crofters' favour, when he visited Skye in 1910 to inquire about the troubles at Idrigil. His boyhood in Glenhinisdale gave him more under-standing of their difficulties than the prosperous Alexander could have had, and his wider reading and greater intellectual gifts illuminated his consideration of practical matters. He expressed his gratitude to his patron's memory by calling his firstborn son after him, though in the softer Gaelic form of Alasdair.

Portree has not changed much in appearance since we lived there as children. It is a composed whole; a piece of town-planning in miniature, contrasting with the wild sweeps of barren moorland or the jagged mountains through which one approaches it from Uig or Broadford. It was

Ronald Macdonald c. 1899.

deliberately placed where it now stands: when Boswell and Johnson crossed the bay from Raasay on Sunday September 12th 1773 they found 'a tolerable inn', and a church where the Rev. Donald MacQueen who was with them officiated in Erse, but otherwise there were only a few scattered huts, and the melancholy presence of an emigrant ship in the bay. Boswell says: 'Sir James Macdonald intended to have built a village here, which would have done great good. A village is like a heart in the country. It produces a perpetual circulation, and gives the people an opportunity to make profit of many little articles which would otherwise be in a good measure lost'. Not much progress had been made by 1819, when a print by William Daniell published by Messrs. Longman depicts a shepherd reclining on the grassy cliff-top where Bosville Terrace now stands, and looking towards an inn and only two other houses above a rough foreshore without pier or jetty. But as the nineteenth century continued the intention was carried out: the tiny capital grew and became the heart of the island. Less than a town but more than a village, it is the only compact planned centre in Skye, as Broadford and Uig are scattered rural communities. It has a situation of unrivalled beauty, on a sheltered bay closed in dramatically by the cliffs of Beal Point on one side, while on the other Ben Tianavaig rises from sea-level to 1350 feet; between them the island of Raasay can be seen beyond the tidal reef of the Black Rock. The village looks inward and eastward, but one cannot forget the dark majesty of the Cuillin Hills dominating the southern bay beyond the Glenvarigill river, or the strange pinnacles of Storr looming to the north. The coastline curves like a sycamore leaf from the Scorrybreck burn to the cliffs and small headland where Redcliffe House is situated, then in another curve to the inner haven with the pier and jetty. Trees grow among the terraces of stone houses that enclose the harbour, and the road ascends steeply to the main town with Somerled Square, Wentworth Street and Bosville Terrace — all the street-names are associated with the Macdonalds of the Isles. I remember it as a grey little town seen from the Scorrybreck cliffs or from below the tower on the Lump; now the houses have been painted soft cream-colour or off-white, so that it lies among the russet moors and hills like a handful of sea-worn shells in a coign of the rocks.

When we lived there the population was about a thousand: the town contained a courthouse and prison, three banks, a combined primary and secondary school, three hotels, a post-office, a Territorial drill-hall, the Skye gathering hall, six churches, and a number of shops, including a baker, a chemist, a draper, J. G. Mackay's hardware store, Mr. Maclean's stationery and toy-shop, and Miss MacArthur's sweetie-shop, magnetic to all the children of the place. All over Skye there were 'big houses' whose tenants often spent the winter in the south and came to the island in summer for shooting and fishing; there were several such houses in Portree: Scorrybreck House, Portree House, Viewfield, Redcliffe, and of course the Lodge.

This is now the Coolin Hills Hotel, but in our day it was the centre from which Lady Macdonald of the Isles rained influence. Her husband was a permanent invalid; her son Archibald had been killed in the Boer War, and her son Godfrey was married in 1908. Armadale Castle, the Regency Gothic mansion in the south of Skye erected by Alexander, the second baron, was becoming too large and expensive for residence by Lady Macdonald and her daughter the Honourable Miss Iona. The Lodge was a dower-house from which she could overlook and stimulate the activities of Portree with the benevolent rule that keeps a community lively, even though it sometimes exasperates individuals. She instituted an annual flower-show with prizes; she gave treats to the school-children and suggested the plan of weekly club-meetings for the country students who were in lodgings. This very great lady was full of simple warm-hearted kindness; when father was in hospital in 1915 and mother with him in London she asked us all to tea, and before we left she gave silver Indian bracelets to Flora and me, and to me as a child fond of reading a book of Scandinavian folk-tales. My impression is that she snatched them from a cabinet and bookcase and gave them with a sudden impulsive generosity.

The National Bank House is no longer a home: it has been much altered, and used only for business. But when we lived there it consisted of two buildings joined together; an old three-storied house at the back, and a new two-storied frontage with higher and more handsome rooms. The back part looked south over the garden and the old graveyard towards an arm of the bay below the ridge of Fingal's Seat: across the shining water we could see from our nursery window the far majestic line of the Black Cuillins, looming through mist or rainstorms, pale iris-blue or dark indigo according to the light of summer days, or with the rose of dawn and sunset lingering on their winter snows. This amazing view was so much part of our lives that it was taken for granted; we found funerals more deeply interesting. We would crowd on to the window-seat to gaze at the coffin and the sad procession of black-clad men — women did not attend funerals in Scotland. Allan recalls that when one of the mourners retired behind a gravestone and took out a handkerchief for a quiet weep, he felt that proper respect had been paid to the departed.

On the ground floor there was a large kitchen with a massive glowing range, a scrubbed wooden table round which the maids used to sit and sing Gaelic songs during the long winter evenings, and a stone floor decorated in curly patterns with whitening after it had been washed. Off this on one side was the scullery with a deep dark sink suitable for scouring iron pots and drawing hens and peeling mountains of potatoes: on another side was the pantry, a more cheerful room where the blue-patterned china was kept and washed, and which contained a locked store-cupboard full of the bags of sugar and flour and oatmeal, the tubs of butter and sides of bacon and barrels of apples that had come by the *Claymore* or the *Clansman* from Glasgow, and which mother dealt out as required. A passage with a swing-

Portree showing the Skye Gathering Hall, the Old Jail, the National Bank House, the Parish Church, and Ross's Royal Hotel.

door led to the dining-room in the new section of the house, papered in dark red, with an oil-painting of Loch Coruisk over the mantelpiece. The rest of the ground floor was occupied by the bank in front with the offices of Macdonald and Fraser behind it. Outside the house was the laundry with deep wooden tubs, a huge boiler built over a coal fire, and a stove for heating flat-irons; here the washing for ten people was done every second week.

On the first floor of the old house the nursery and pink room looked south with the bathroom between them: it had a bath large enough for two children at once, with a high end containing a Shower, Spray, Douche and Plunge to enliven our ablutions. The brown peaty water from below the precipices of Storr was soft as milk and dark as tea in the winter lamplight: shouting with joy we soaped our little rumps and slid down at a rush with the shower going briskly at the other end. Behind these, looking east and west, were the spare-room with its dressing-room, and a room which held a linen-cupboard and some pieces of extra furniture. On the top floor was the maids' bedroom where the housemaid and cook shared a big iron bed, and the attic which was made into our playroom. The nursemaid slept with the children in one of the nurseries. A green carpeted stair with another swing-door led up to the higher and grander rooms in the front of the house. This was a very convenient arrangement; if our parents were entertaining visitors, or beginning to find us tiresome, we could be chased down the green stairs to rampage happily out of earshot in our own quarters.

An impressive feature of the front-house was the red stair with its glowing carpet and polished mahogany rail. It swept up to the three chief rooms; a pretty drawing-room which we used very little; our parents' bedroom, and the beloved library, the centre of all our lives. It had an oriel and a flat sash-window both looking up the wide street above the harbour; round the oriel there was a cushioned seat from which you could observe the life of the town, or, looking east to the side, catch a glimpse of the bay through the trees, and watch for the steamer coming round the point. Another window looked west over the garden, so that the room was full of light, though every wall was lined with books from floor to cornice: one could have become learned in history from the Greeks and Romans onwards; in the whole span of English literature and in a great deal of European literature in translation. There was a grand piano, and a long comfortable sofa on which our tall father could relax when weary, but he usually sat in his own big chair, absorbed in a book, gently puffing his pipe. Mother and father had their own desks, and there was a large table where she plied her sewing-machine on winter evenings, and where Christmas presents were laid out. Cinerarias or geraniums from the greenhouse stood here and there; the fire danced under the white marble mantelpiece and winked on the polished brass of poker and tongs. Here we learned our first lessons, and played card-games or ludo with mother at the table, and had books read to us before bedtime, in perfect happiness and security.

The house was lit by paraffin lamps, which emphasised the difference between the warm illuminated rooms with fires and people, and the dim bogey stairs and passages. There was a small lamp on the nursery landing, a large one on the front hall stand, and one on a table outside the library but all around were doors opening on dark lairs, and corridors from which beasts might spring. Newspapers were delivered late in the evening after the boat had come in, and it was an act of real courage to volunteer when father asked, 'Who'll go for my *Scotsman*?' — especially in winter when storms were thundering round the house and rain lashing on the staircase window. All alone one crept down the red stairs, holding one's breath across the shadowy half-landing. The hall was well-lit, but one had to open the front door to the roaring chaos of blackness outside, seize the paper with its smell of rain and printers' ink, slam the door against the pushing arms of the gale, and run madly upstairs again, with demons shouting all round and dangers with claws lurking in the unlit passage.

Morning came, and we ran out to play in the garden with its tall old pear-tree which flowered but did not fruit, and was perfect for climbing. We had our own special perches, and asked permission to visit one another. The climate seemed to discourage the few apple and pear trees which never bore very much, but favoured soft fruit and vegetables, so that we had a large strawberry bed, rows of raspberries, and a whole plantation of luscious gooseberries bordered by red and black currant bushes. There was a wealth of flowers; deep dewy roses; columbines self sown everywhere; pæonies and tall tiger-lilies; snapdragons, penstemons and marigolds at the end of summer, and great bushes of philadelphus and flowering currant. Willie Ross, our gardener, had a toolshed smelling of earth and tarry twine where carrots were stored in bins of sand under the stagings; we crept in and took a few for a delicious gritty crunch. All round the garden ran a wall covered with ivy; we climbed on to it and crawled along, daring each other to walk upright. Then we dropped down on the other side to the overgrown graveyard, to read inscriptions and admire china wreaths under glass bells, and discuss how we would like to be buried when our time came.

Besides the garden and the graveyard there was the Lump just round the corner. This hideous name desecrates a beautiful wooded headland which juts into the bay between the pier and the mouth of the Leasgeary. From the village street a track rises gently towards the green circle of an arena from which had been quarried the stone for the Skye Gathering Hall, and several commodious houses in the Square. Here the Skye Games were held, and here a solemn inter-denominational service for King Edward VII took place in 1910. On the highest point of the hill a small tower has been erected, a romantic feature skilfully placed to catch the eye from afar and emphasise the steep rise of the headland from the sea. In our time a well-kept path ran all round the promontory some height above the bay, shaded by beeches and pines, and there was a track at sea-level; now the path has fallen away in places, and the track has almost disappeared. Great thickets of rhododendron and occasional laburnums had been planted among the native trees; in spring there were drifts of wild hyacinths and clusters of primroses and violets above the sea. This was our scramble-course and adventure-playground: we had houses and dens in the rhododendron clumps, and practised climbing among the cliffs, and here we had our fort, a jutting ledge of rock with turf bastions built all round it, and stores of pine-cones for ammunition, and an armoury of bows and arrows.

After our parents, our most beloved person was Atten, the name we gave to Catriona Cameron, mother's dearest friend. When I was learning to speak, mother wanted me to call her Auntie, and thought I had mastered the word, but when I was sent to welcome her and to display my new accomplishment, I came staggering down the red stairs, holding out my arms and saying 'Atten! Atten!' The name seemed more appropriate to someone who was not really a relation, so we kept it. She was very tiny and slight; a grown-up who was almost on child-level for kisses and hugs. She wore her hair in a queue tied up with a velvet ribbon, and had dark blue eyes and a quick light voice and a quiet glancing sense of humour. Her aunt Miss Maclachlan, with whom she lived in a little two-storied house in Bosville Terrace overlooking the bay, died in 1911, and after that she often spent Sundays with us, coming after church for mid-day dinner which we had with our parents on that day. She had a maid called Agnes, and one of the lady-teachers from the school generally boarded with her; she also gave piano-lessons to pupils in the village, and towards the end of our stay in Skye, Alasdair and I came to her as beginners. He was a musical little boy and made good progress, but I must have been a trial to her. All the same, I was her special child though she loved us all: if ever I suffered from the natural stresses of family life I could be sure of gentle understanding and consideration in Atten's little house. Her name for me was 'treasure'.

Mother wrote to our grandmother every week on Sunday evenings. After her children had gone to bed she sat down at her desk and rapidly covered eight sides or more of folded octavo-size paper in her small fluent handwriting. We had just had our weekly Bible-lesson, so she often gives an amused account of our reaction to moral teaching or to Old Testament characters. It is obvious that we were well-grounded in the Scriptures, and that our parents' deeply-held Christian beliefs were carefully imparted. This loving conscientious teaching gave us an anchorage for which we have always been grateful; we were fortunate also that our home had no trace of the gloomy Sabbatarianism that frequently oppressed Scottish children at that period, especially in Skye.

   'We can't for a certainty tell
     What mirth may molest us on Monday;
   But at least, to begin the week well,
     Let us all be unhappy on Sunday.'

But for us Sunday was the joyful day when we had dinner and tea with our parents, with specially delicious food, and a feeling of leisure and mutual appreciation. There were no solemn airs, and the only limit to our play in the garden was that we must not shout too loudly and disturb the congregations in the churches that unfortunately neighboured us on two sides. A cloud on the horizon came when we were taken to church ourselves, which happened when we were still of tender years. Even mother's cheerful spirit was daunted by the chill of the church and the long dreariness of the service. Still, she had her sense of humour to uphold her, and no doubt she could glean inspiration here and there from the readings or sermon. Grown-ups have mental resources of memory and association denied to children. Lacking these, we suffered agonies of cramp and boredom; I would have emphatically agreed with Matthew Arnold when he described the Presbyterian service as 'the most dismal performance ever invented by man'. The metrical psalms with their stilted metres and lugubrious tunes had no hint of the word-harmonies of their great originals; the extempore prayers rambled on with monotonous forced emphasis, and the sermon seemed endless, until I was allowed to read my Bible as it droned on over my head, and discovered the Song of Solomon, and the Revelation of St John the Divine.

It may seem strange that in a small community like Portree with only a thousand people there should be six separate churches. As well as the Episcopalian church and the tiny Catholic chapel there were four different varieties of Presbyterianism: besides the United Free church in the Square which we attended, there was the Established Church on one side of the National Bank, the United Presbyterians on the approach to the Lump, and the Free Presbyterians also in the Square. The last-named were fervent Calvinists and strict Sabbatarians, very gloomy and godly. they disapproved of our church soirée, and their minister would not allow the people of Braes to have a concert in their school because he sometimes held a service there. It was probably a member of that congregation who had scruples about making a fire for Atten in her aunt's sickroom on a Sunday. But it was difficult to find any important difference of doctrine or discipline between the other three: their separation was due to the peculiarly fissiparous character of Scottish Presbyterianism. The Established Church could claim to be the nearest thing to a state church in Scotland, but its influence in Skye was small because in 1843 when the great Disruption took place on the question of patronage, most of the ministers 'came out' to form the Free Church. In 1847 a number of the sects which had split off in the eighteenth or early nineteenth centuries either joined the Free Church, which then became the United Free, or joined together to form the United Presbyterian Church. A small group left the Free Church in protest against this receiving of other sheep which were not of the fold, and called themselves Free Presbyterians, but the group of this name in Skye was born from a schism which took place in the United Free Church in 1892, led by the Rev. Donald Macfarlane of Raasay. Dr. Norman Maclean gives an interesting eye-witness account of the beginning of this secession in his book *Set Free*, though it is difficult to make out just what they were seceding about with such determination, or to understand why he, as a minister of the Established Church, should have found yet another schism so admirable. 'The minister prayed', he says with no hint of irony, 'that the Spirit of the Disruption might be poured out again on this Island so favoured by God in the past'. Evidently his prayer did not go unheard. In 1900 formal union took place in most of Scotland between the United Free and the United Presbyterian churches, but in Portree they continued as separate congregations under the Rev. Norman Macleod and the Rev. Mr. Davidson. When Mr. Davidson left to go to Whithorn in Wigtownshire it seemed only common sense to unite these two small groups of Presbyterians, as had been done in the rest of the country. But from mother's letters it can be seen that this was far from easy.

The only outstanding difference between the two congregations in Portree was that the U.P.s sang an occasional hymn to an harmonium during their services, while the U.F.s confined themselves to the metrical psalms led by a precentor. The objection to hymns among the stricter Presbyterians is that they are the words of man, not the words of God like the Psalms of David, but it is difficult to discern the words of God in the shambling bathos of the merical version; besides, unless hymns are allowed, a Christian congregation is forbidden to sing the praise of Christ. The same strange reasoning prohibited the use of the Lord's Prayer in some Presbyterian churches because it is a set form, and all public prayer must be extempore. Poor mother did not ask for much; only a few cheerful hymns like those sung in the Baptist congregation of her girlhood, and a sensible direct sermon that she could apply to her daily life. However, when Mr Macleod died in 1912 the congregations were at last united under Mr. Morrison, an energetic young minister with modern ideas: soon hymns were being sung and babies christened in church, and no one raised any objections.

The family at Glenhinisdale was strongly attached to the Free Presbyterian body, especially Aunt Catriona and our grandmother. She was a gentle devout old woman, but it was difficult for us to know her well, as she spoke very little English. In Scottish Presbyterian churches Holy Communion was celebrated only twice a year: in Portree it was in March and in August, and to prepare worshippers for the sacrament long services were held for several days. Her visits to Portree for the Communion must have been great occasions in Glen Grannie's life, and her endurance was remarkable, though mother was always anxious about the effect on her health of five-hour services and irregular meals. Because the sacrament was celebrated so rarely it was attended with extreme and perhaps over-scrupulous reverence: only those who led lives of outstanding holiness were allowed to take communion, and since humility is the breath of holiness, such people often abstained from a sense of their own unworthiness. It might be said that the piety of a congregation was measured by the fewness of its communicants rather than by their number. Dr. Maclean, describing an open-air celebration at Sconser, says 'There were about fifteen communicants and over a hundred worshippers'; and he quotes an old man as saying, 'The two best persons I ever knew, my own father and mother, never communicated'. So, after her many hours of prayer and worship, my Highland grandmother may not ever have received Holy Communion.

As well as being a centre of religious diversity, Portree was an important junction in West Highland communications. The great Glasgow shipping firm of David MacBrayne is still responsible for the passenger and goods services that link the islands with each other and with the mainland, but in these days when roads were poor and motor travel costly, their boats were the quickest, and often the only, way of getting from one part of Skye to another. The road that now runs by the two small lochs and under the cliffs of Storr to Staffin, continuing round the Trotternish wing of the island to Uig, was just being made: on Saturday afternoons father sometimes took us for the long walk to one of the lochs to inspect its progress. So when Annie took Allan home with her they would go by the *Lapwing* which left Portree at 6 a.m. on three mornings a week, called at Staffin and Kilmaluag, then went round the north of Skye to Tarbert and Rodel in Harris. When father went to Lochmaddy in North Uist to attend the inquiry into the Vatersay squatters' case in November 1909 he went by the *Plover* or the *Lochiel*, one of which left Oban on alternate days, and made a long circular trip, by Tobermory, Rum and Canna, then up the west side of Skye to Struan in Bracadale, Loch Pooltiel in Glendale, and Dunvegan, from which it would cross to the Outer Isles, taking in both Uists and Barra before returning to Oban. The other boat went to Barra first and made the same calls in reverse order. The *Lapwing*, *Plover* and *Lochiel* were sturdy little single-screw steamers with black hulls and scarlet funnels topped by a band of black: they went to and fro all the year round by the gull's way and the whale's way, into sea lochs and between islands, keeping a schedule that might be elastic as to exact times of arrival but was faithful to days of the week, and carrying mail, passengers and cargo, with some distress to bad travellers when Atlantic tempests were stirring, but with an unspoiled record of safety and reliability.

But the steamers we knew best were the *Glencoe* and the *Gael* which connected the mainland ports of Mallaig and Kyle of Lochalsh with Portree. The *Glencoe* which made the winter run was the oldest boat in the line, built in 1846 and originally called the *Mary Jane*. She was a marine curiosity, a small squat paddle boat with an obsolete steeple-engine that darted up and down in a shed on the deck. Accommodation was limited: there was a stuffy dining-saloon downstairs with a gilded eagle poised over its entrance, a cramped ladies' cabin on deck, and as she sailed in Scottish waters there probably was a bar somewhere. Fortunately her route lay in comparatively sheltered waters on the east side of Skye by Broadford and Raasay; she did not have to venture across the Minch like the *Plover* or the *Lapwing*. Even so she sometimes could not call at Mallaig in rough weather: then passengers would take the Stornoway boat, the *Sheila*, to Kyle, where they could transfer to the *Glencoe*, as Nurse Macfadyen did before Flora's birth. The *Sheila* was a single-screw steamer that called at Wester Ross ports but did not visit Portree.

Besides these smaller boats built chiefly for passengers and mail the islands were served by the MacBrayne cargo-steamers from Glasgow, the *Claymore*, the *Clansman* and the *Chieftain*. These were strong finely-proportioned ships that made the journey from Glasgow to Stornoway, taking a week in either direction and connecting a very large number of small ports. But in really stormy weather even these strongly-built vessels found difficulty in making their piers and ferries, which is probably why Mr. Thomson's factor in November 1914 was unable to land at Eigg and was even carried past Mallaig and Kyle to Portree where he would have to wait for the boat's return from Stornoway.

So it can be seen that an intricate network of MacBrayne steamer-routes connected the scattered archipelagoes of the Outer and Inner Hebrides at that time when the islands were more thickly populated and other forms of transport did not exist. The sight of the red funnel appearing round a rocky point; the slanting course of the dark hull towards the pier, or the warning hoot and the rush of steam as the engines slowed and the ship lay rocking on the waves, side-hatch open towards the labouring ferry-boat — these must have been central events of the day in numerous tiny communities of crofters marooned among lochs and mountains. The unique position of this firm in the Highlands is expressed in the parody of the metrical psalm chanted by children along the Firth of Clyde at the end of the nineteenth century:-

'The earth belongs unto the Lord,
With all that it contains:
Except the Scottish Western Isles,
And they are D. MacBrayne's.'

During the period of the letters, motor cars gradually came into common use. In 1908 when we went on an excursion to Uig 'to blow away the dregs of the whooping-cough' we travelled in a horse-drawn vehicle, but on future occasions we went by car. Father's business took him all over the island, and he often made an outing of it with his family if the weather was good and he was going to some interesting place. A car was hired for the day with a driver: they were still so expensive that only rich people could be private owners. There was very little protection from the elements: none at all, apparently, in the luxurious Sunbeam that carried father and mother through the Cuillins from Duisdale in a November hailstorm. The front seat was high like that of a carriage, which explains why Allan fell out on the road between Drynoch bridge and Sligachan when the two little boys were sitting beside the driver and the car swerved. Around 1912 Mr. Macdonald of the Home Farm started a regular motor mail-service between Portree and Uig. A great lumbering char-a-banc with several rows of seats and room for luggage and packages left from outside the post-office every evening after the letters had been sorted. It went snorting off in clouds of exhaust, and the sound of its labours as it dragged itself up Drumuie Brae could be heard all over the district, but it was a very convenient innovation, especially for us, as it passed the end of Glenhinisdale.

Other indispensables of modern civilisation make their first appearances in the letters: there is the thermos flask which is so expensive that father and mother club together to buy it as an extravagant joint Christmas present. Our delight in the gramophone that we were given in 1912 is vividly described; we had so few entertainments of any kind that this wonder-box which sang to us at will was like magic. And in 1911 mother hires and tries out a primitive form of vacuum-cleaner; it was worked by hand and was very exhausting to use, but it saved the labour of carrying the carpets out to be beaten in the rain that invariably accompanied spring-cleaning, and indeed a good deal of our lives. It must be remembered that the rainfall in Skye is just over 71 inches per annum: in London it is about 23 inches.

Throughout the letters the characters of her children are vividly realised. I was a difficult child; strong-willed and argumentative, sometimes perverse and sometimes tearful; in fact before the letters began I had nearly driven mother to despair with tantrums, malice and refusal to eat. Displacement-shock at the birth of a new baby was not so well understood then as it is now, and my behaviour after Alasdair had arrived looked like an inexplicable outburst of original sin or even mania, giving rise to grave fears for my future. But the storms died down and further additions to the family were accepted with interest; indeed I can remember my exquisite joy when Flora was put into my arms on the day she was born, a light warm little bundle with a tiny puss-soft face for a first kiss. After that forgotten time of inarticulate resentment I had the great good fortune to develop, as a child of sensitive imagination, amid the greatest natural beauty, laughed at and loved, in a house full of books.

Alasdair was a kind hearted thoughtful little boy, yet strong-minded enough to resist his domineering elder sister. At school he found himself in his element, not only because of the ease with which he sailed through the Standards, but because his happy affable nature expanded into comradeship with other boys. He was not particular; if a boy was good company and ready for fun it did not matter if he wore a ragged jersey or had a dirty face or ran barefoot for much of the year. Toys or cigarette-cards were generously handed over in the family if he thought they would give pleasure, then the untidy tousle-headed eager little figure would rush out with trailing boot-laces to join his friends. In contrast, Allan's interest in neatness and in attractive new clothes appears very early: he had more sense of his own personality and appearance than Alasdair had. Yet he was never self-conscious or conceited: his sea-blue eyes looked out on the world with happy expectation, and he often vibrated from head to foot in a wordless dance of joy. One never knew what he would do next in the way of experiment: he was found with an empty poison-bottle in his hand; he tried to pour paraffin on the nursery fire; he cut off Flora's hair, and he put his celluloid collar round the funnel of a lighted lamp 'just to see what would happen'.

After having whooping cough at six weeks old poor Flora was never very strong, and during her seven years she had to fight her way through several serious illnesses, yet she is seen to have a quiet resilience after each; in fact 'quiet' is the adjective most often applied to this gentle child in contrast to the more spirited personalities around her. Even Peter, our dark-haired elfin little fosterling made more noise, stamping joyously about the house or shouting with rage when we teased him.

Compared to these vividly-drawn pictures our father appears rather shadowy, a silent though not unconcerned figure in the background. 'He reads books', Alasdair had said after long thought when asked what his father did. Naturally mother took him for granted in her letters more than she did her children who were developing every week like plants under glass. He was somewhat inarticulate: letters of his that have been kept are written in a stiff conventional English which contrasts with her gay ease of expression. But his love for his island, his wife and his children was so deeply rooted that when he was sent far into exile in 1916 he died.

'Children of the mist,
Come and be kissed!'

he would call to us as he came into the library, and we rushed into his arms. Our long walks over the hills were sometimes a test of stamina, but he took us because he wanted us to share from our earliest years his passion for the great lines of the mountains, the views of sea and island: a more selfish man would have enjoyed these alone without a pack of children trailing at his heels. When we came to a stream too wide for us to cross easily he would take each child by an arm and a leg, and after two or three swings would toss it into the springy clumps of honey-dusted heather on the other side: we loved the sense of his strength and the wonderful moment of flight. He taught me to recognise trees as mother did flowers, and we shared poetry. I especially remember his saying *The Burial of Sir John Moore at Corunna* to me in his deep voice as we walked by the Scorrybreck shore one autumn dusk.

'But he lay like a warrior taking his rest,
With his martial cloak around him.'

There are a few letters from 1907, but the regular weekly series begins in 1908 when I am four years old, Alasdair two, Allan one, and Flora about to make her appearance in February. She was not called directly after the Skye heroine, but after Glen Grannie who had been Flora Mathieson, though the naming of so many Highland girl-children after the Roman goddess of flowers was started by the tacksman in South Uist who gave his baby daughter that alien and poetic name in 1722. Our nurse was Annie MacLean from Culnancnock, Staffin, who came when Allan was born and loved him dearly. She was a very responsible and trustworthy girl, and could be left in charge of the babies when mother went south. She stayed with us for six years, and was so fond of small children that twice she took one home with her for her holiday. Bella was the housemaid who put the children to bed on Annie's afternoon off and helped to take them for walks, and the cook was Lexy, a Raasay girl who had met so few germs on her remote island that she was always catching infectious diseases. Mama, our name for mother, is pronounced with the accent on the first syllable.

1908—New Baby: Yacht Cruise: Dunvegan Wedding

The letters begin in October 1907 with an account of my inconveniently vigorous imagination. Like many children I had an imaginary playmate, a little girl called Susie who was a more intelligent companion than the baby brothers, and could be blamed for all my misdeeds. At that time I was so surrounded by invisible children and animals that poor Annie must have found me very tiresome: if she sat down on a chair the nursery might echo with screams of rage because she was sitting on Susie or on Betsey the Cow. No wonder we did not get on very well; she had never met anything like this in Staffin. On coming home one afternoon from paying a call mother found two-year-old Alasdair in a state of panic.

'He clung to me, and kept looking at the door saying, "Addie frightened for a man with a tail: a man with a tail come in at the door and bite Addie". I saw that the child was really frightened, and asked Isobel what he meant. Thereupon she began a long yarn that whenever you leave a door open a man with a tail comes in. If it is shut he can't come in because he has no arms and can't open it. And one day Susie saw him. She heard the baby crying, and when she ran to see what the matter was, there was the man with the tail standing beside it, and the poor wee arm was all bleeding where he had bitten it. I told her that she must not tell stories like that to Alasdair; that there were no men with tails; then she threw herself on the floor in her own excited fashion, declaring that it *wasn't* a story, that Susie had told her, and Susie had *seen* the man, and she must tell Alasdair what Susie tells her. I said she was not to tell Alasdair anything that frightened him, whether Susie told her or not. There the matter ended, but tonight Alasdair carefully shut the door after him to keep the man with the tail out. I questioned the girls, but none of them were telling her tales, and she sees no one but ourselves'.

Mother remarks in this letter that Miss Milne, a teacher at Portree school was leaving the island. 'She has been appointed language mistress at Fordyce Academy at £120 a year. I shall miss her very much'. Evidently the well-qualified Miss Milne was considered lucky to earn such an excellent salary.

Alasdair was a chubby little boy with soft fair hair. 'He came to me the other day with an offended air, saying, "A lady called Addie a Fatty! Addie not like that. Addie not a Fatty. Addie a nice wee boy". So you see he has sensitive feelings'. We were all demonstrative children, given to warm hugs and kisses when we felt fond of each other, and to tooth-and-nail combat when our interests clashed. Mother teasingly passed the blame to father by referring to our 'Celtic temperaments'.

'Isobel has been bearing the marks this week of Alasdair's Celtic temperament. They have both — indeed all — a bit of the Celt in them, with the result that when they disagree they fly at each other like little savages. You can imagine my feelings when the kind lady takes the nice little girl on her knee and asks, "Has the cat been scratching you, my dear?" and she replies with cheerful alacrity, "Oh no, it was Alasdair did it". If the kind lady has no children of her own she looks very shocked. They are pretty well-matched now for strength, and though Alasdair has an amiable disposition he will not be imposed upon. They are playing very nicely together now, all the same, and are really very fond of each other'.

Towards the end of January mother, eight months pregnant, cheerfully took sole charge of her three children to let Annie off from Tuesday till Monday to attend a wedding in the isle of Raasay which lies outside Portree harbour, between Skye and the mainland. North of it is Rona, a small and rocky island with a lighthouse on its outermost tip. Both Raasay and Rona were much more thickly populated than they are now, but the houses were primitive and the roads between them mere tracks, so a January wedding in West Highland weather must have been something of an endurance test for all concerned.

'The rain has been coming down almost unceasingly since last Sunday, and I have been nowhere. The children have only been twice out of doors all week, for unlike Robert in *Strewelpeter* we do not think that "when it pours, it is better out of doors", and so, like good bairns, we "all stay at home and mind our toys". In my case it is rather, stay at home and mind my boys, especially when Annie is away. We have got on very well without her, and I really have not missed her much, though I shall be glad to see her home again tomorrow night. I am longing to hear what her adventures were. I told you she was going to a wedding in Raasay where she was to be best maid. As far as I can make out it takes about a week to get married in Raasay, and with weather like this and the long distances they have to walk from one place to another it must be a cheery affair! Tuesday, the day Annie went off, was one of unceasing, pitiless, relentless rain. The sky seemed to rest on top of the trees and houses and empty its contents without mercy. Annie went over with the minister in the morning boat, and was going to get breakfast in Lexy's mother's house and then proceed to the church where she was to meet the rest of the bridal party. They meanwhile had to walk seven miles of a footpath. Annie had three miles to go to the church, and then after the ceremony they all had to trudge the seven miles back again through the rain. It seems that in Raasay old customs still prevail, and, however young a bride is, she must be married in a bonnet and black cape. The bridesmaid is also supposed to wear a bonnet, but Annie struck at that and bought a new hat with a feather in it. I wonder what the bonnet and the feather were like at the end of a fourteen mile tramp!

'After they got home there would be a feast, I suppose, and then dancing till five or six next morning in the bride's house. Wednesday was also to be spent there with more festivities. On Thursday the bride and bridegroom,

Annie and the best man were to proceed to Rona where his parents lived and where the young couple were to take up house. So again in the pouring rain they would have to walk three miles to the north end of Raasay, cross to Rona in a boat and walk another three miles to their destination where there would be another feast of welcome home from the Rona folk. Next day they were to cross the island to the lighthouse where there were to be more festivities. Then today came the kirking, also in pouring rain, and tomorrow Annie must be up early, walk three miles in Rona, then cross over to Raasay and walk another thirteen miles to the steamer to get home by tomorrow night. After that I think she will want a day in bed before she is fit for much work. If the bride and bridegroom get through all that without losing their tempers they will surely have a chance of living happily ever after!'

In two of the letters there are glimpses of our tall studious father. 'Ronald has been deeply interested this week in the three bulky volumes of Queen Victoria's letters which were lent him by Sheriff Campbell. I expect to most people they would be a trifle heavy, for no one could charge our good queen, however well-equipped she was in other respects, of being over-burdened with either imagination or humour. But Ronald has the political history of the times so thoroughly at his finger-ends that he has greatly enjoyed them'.

And a week later. 'Ronald is busy at present preparing his annual paper for the Literary Society, and is up to his eyes in books. His subject is "Dugald Dalgetty" It seems that Scott drew his inspiration for this character from two soldiers of fortune who fought under Gustavus Adolphus and both left memoirs. It would seem to you or me an easy enough matter to compose a paper from the novel and these materials, but not so to Ronald. To him it involves the study of European history for at least half a century, including a minute study of the biographies of all the leading men. It means the arrival of huge parcels of out-of-the-way books from the London and other libraries, and the purchase of one rare book, the price of which he refuses to reveal to the wife of his bosom. Dear Ronald! I wonder if either of his sons will be like him when they grow up. His little daughter certainly is, as he himself admitted the other day. I was trying to show her the error of her ways when my persuasive eloquence was nipped in the bud by a passionate little voice exclaiming, "Mama, don't be arguing with *Me*!" It was so like her Daddy's attitude on certain occasions that it made him smile. She finds it difficult to take correction in the proper spirit, though she has not needed quite so much of it lately, I am glad to say. She has been very good and happy, making songs and lullabies and composing prayers which is her latest fad. They are queer mixtures in which the beauties of nature and the virtues of her dollies are described. I must try to capture one some day and send it to you'.

And next week mother does get hold of a prayer in which I took as determined a line with God as I did with my elders and betters.

'Isobel is still at her prayers. The other day I heard one which began in very pious tones,
    "Jesus! Jesus! Jesus!
    Keep me safe tonight".

I don't know how it went on as I was not listening particularly, but it ended with the words, "And take my advice", in a much less pious tone. It occurred to me that the "Amen" at the end of the prayers of some older people has much the same meaning, though not expressed in so many words'.

This letter was written on February 16th, eight days before Flora's birth. As her eldest child was only four years and six months old and there was only one year and two months between Flora and Allan, mother was afraid that Grannie would be alarmed at this rapid succession of babies, so did not let her know that another was on the way. But Grannie began to wonder why Lizzie was leading such a quiet life: there had been no news of parties or even of visits for a long time. Casting an eye over her figure, and chuckling at the thought of going to dances and entertainments in her advanced condition, mother replied:-

'You were asking me if I don't get time for recreation. I'm afraid I can't send you accounts of balls and dinner-parties, but I must say I feel very little inclination at present to trip the light fantastic toe, less than ever I did, so I am not mourning over the lack of opportunity. I expect to have a nice holiday soon, next month perhaps, but you shall hear more of that later'.

The next news was a telegram sent to Grannie on February 24th that must have startled her considerably. It was followed by a letter from father apologising for the surprise, and explaining that it had been Lizzie's idea to save worry. She had had a comparatively easy time: the doctor was sent for after 1 p.m. and the little girl arrived at 2.45. We had all been sent off for a walk with Annie to get us out of the way: it was bitterly cold with flurries of snow, and we were taken further along the Sligachan road than we had ever gone before. Our little legs failed us: Alasdair began to cry with cold and weariness and was lifted into the pram beside Allan, but I had to plod endlessly as Annie loitered along to fill in time. At last we turned and made our slow way back. In the village we met a lady who said, 'Guess what's happened at home — you've got a little sister!' 'What nonsense!' I thought. 'A grown-up making a silly joke'. I was cross and cold and tired, and in no mood for happy surprises, but when we came in by the back door to the warm kitchen Lexy was sitting by the fire, and she said the same thing. I believed it then, and soon I was taken up to see mother in bed, and hold in my arms a tiny thing that blinked and moved and made little whimpering noises.

But mother nearly had her baby without the comfort of a nurse. Father says in his letter:- 'The weather on Saturday was terrible here, and we had very little hope of the steamer being able to call at Mallaig, and did not expect the nurse to arrive. The Stornoway boat, however, was able to call at Mallaig although the Portree boat was not, and brought the Portree passengers, including Nurse Macfadyen to Kyle where they joined the *Glencoe* which arrived at Portree about two and a half hours late.' Flora was born on a Monday, so the nurse had a day to recover from her stormy voyage before going on duty, but getting a maternity nurse to Portree was a chancy business. If the baby arrived early she might not be there in time, and if it was late she might have to leave soon after the birth. Flora's arrival could not have been better timed, but Allan kept everyone waiting till almost the end of the nurse's stay. It was in bleak December too, and mother once told me how she and the nurse sat wearily together evening after evening, and the time drifted on towards Christmas. 'I don't think this baby is *ever* going to be born!' she would cry despairingly as yet another day drew to a close. 'There's nothing surer', the nurse would reply, looking shrewdly over her patient.

The new baby was a plump pretty little thing, and the nurse, who had been ward sister for three years in a maternity hospital, was pleasant and capable. Mother looked forward to a good rest in bed and a holiday from household cares. She writes of her other children: 'Isobel is greatly delighted with her little sister. Alasdair is too, though more moderately, but the wee black head and red face strike only terror into the heart of baby Allan. He seems to think she is a new species of monkey that might jump on him at any moment'.

Allan was a bold and active child: his new-born sister was the only thing that ever frightened him, but unlike the other two he had not seen anything like her before. A week later he begins to accept her. 'Allan has become more reconciled to Baby this week, and looks at her with grave interest. He even solemnly kisses her, but he still stands a good deal in awe of her. He has just been in to see me, and has been climbing all over the chairs. I don't see much of him as he is too stirring to be left alone for a moment, but I have the other two in and out constantly, and they keep me cheery'.

During the third week of March when mother was beginning to get up for part of the day, Lexy the maid from Raasay developed a severe cold, and the two oldest children seemed to have caught it. There was a good deal of whooping-cough about, so the doctor was called in who suspected the worst, and sure enough, in a few days Lexy was 'crowing away in fine style'. There was no doubt that we were all in for it.

Every effort was made to keep the infection from the month-old baby. The nurse was asked to stay on for another week, and to isolate herself with the child in the big front bedroom while mother cut short her convalescence and went down to the back part of the house which soon resounded with whoops. Fortunately within a week she found a new nurse for the baby; 'an elderly woman who had had thirty years' experience of nursing children of all ages in good families. She was disengaged and staying with a sister in Portree: she was quite willing to come until she heard of another situation'. This was Nurse Chisholm described by mother as 'thin and grey, with Features and an Air'. We were lucky to get such an experienced and reliable person to take sole charge of the baby, though later her aristocratic memories made her a somewhat dissatisfied and critical member of an ordinary middle-class household.

But Flora had been with the other children, being hugged and kissed tenderly during their infectious period before the illness had been diagnosed, and in spite of all precautions, early in April when she was barely six weeks old, it became clear that she had whooping-cough. Mother had missed her badly during the isolation weeks. 'I am not allowed to go near baby at all. You can imagine what a trial it is to hear her cry and not be able to go to her'. Now there was a joyful reunion. 'How glad I was to get baby into my arms again! It almost took away the sting of the whooping-cough. She cooed and laughed when I took her as if she was glad to come to me'. As for the illness, she fought her way through it. 'It is strange to hear a tiny baby having such fits of coughing and whooping, but she is a strong wee creature, and I think she will worry through'.

Early in May we were back to our normal health again, and mother was ready to go on with my religious education. I had the fresh unstrained, untrained memory of a young child, and she was surprised to find how retentive it could be. 'The Sunday before baby was born I read her out of *Line upon Line* the account of the first six plagues of Egypt. Her next Bible lesson was four weeks later. I asked her if she remembered what her last lesson was about; she not only remembered, but could tell me five of the six plagues in their right order. When I remembered the blank looks of my old Sunday School scholars when I asked them to tell what the lesson was that I had tried so dramatically to impress upon them the Sunday before, I can't help thinking she has an extra good memory'. Alas! It would be useless to ask me today to recite the plagues of Egypt in their correct order, and I have forgotten many other things that would be more profitable to remember.

Then Alasdair and I were taken on a delightful excursion to Uig, that scattered township in north-west Skye that looks across the Minch to Harris and Uist. Its fields are green and the crofts around the bay are fertile; it looks like a garden to travellers arriving from the stony Outer Isles. We went in a horse-drawn carriage which made a slow business of the fifteen miles between Uig and Portree, and as it was open to the weather the drive home in the rain must have been dreary enough. Both mother and father wore Inverness capes of solid tweed like snug tents under which children could nestle and sleep.

'Friday was the Portree spring holiday, and as Ronald had business in Uig he proposed taking Atten and me, and Isobel and Alasdair to blow away the dregs of the whooping-cough. You can imagine how excited the children were, especially Alasdair, who has never been out of Portree since he was nine months old. He has a book of natural history with pictures of wild animals which he is very fond of, and he was constantly expecting to meet the most extraordinary animals such as zebras, pampas-cats and musk-deer, not to mention a hippinabotomus. He answered someone who asked him if he would not rather walk to Uig by saying, "Oh no! Addie might meet a monkey and it would eat him all up". As our friend had not thought of monkeys being one of the dangers of the Uig road he was much amused. However we got safely to Uig without meeting anything out of the way, and how the children enjoyed the drive! Ronald went to his meeting, and we made our way to the woods and the burn and had a little picnic while the bairns ran about in glee. Then we went back to the hotel for dinner, where Alasdair distinguished himself by the amount of food he consumed and the gusto with which he consumed it. After dinner we climbed the hill to the peaceful graveyard where Grandfather Macdonald is buried. A new stone had been erected: it looked very well with its Celtic carvings. When we got back to the hotel the bairns went off with the driver to see the horses at their dinner while we had a cup of tea. By now it was time to go home, and rain was beginning to fall. We got very wet, but the bairns were covered with shawls. Soon Alasdair was sound asleep under Daddy's cloak, and slept all the way home'.

In June Annie went off for a well-earned holiday in Staffin, and the children were put in charge of old Nurse Chisholm who had been engaged to look after Flora in the whooping-cough crisis, and had stayed on with the baby in her sole care, occupying the large front bedroom while mother and father were exiled to the spare bedroom at the back. But her 'thirty years' experience of nursing children of all ages in good families' did not help her to cope with the little Macdonalds. Her nerves were shattered by the noise of the three rioting individualists in her care. she much preferred a room to herself and one quiet little baby, and mother was made uneasy by the atmosphere of long-suffering and reproach that could be felt in the nursery.

However Annie came back in July, and then our parents were free to enjoy a short period of high life; they went cruising with Sir Donald and Lady Currie. Sir Donald (1825-1909) was founder and chairman of the Union Castle Line which connected England with South Africa. He had been a Liberal M.P. for Perthshire where he owned two estates; he also rented the island of Scalpay, south of Raasay, where he made Scalpay House a base for cruises in his outsize steam yacht the *Iolaire*. The name is Gaelic for 'eagle'. It was like a small liner, gleaming white with yellow funnels and rows of portholes and windows. It must have needed a large crew of sailors, stokers and stewards to run it, as well as its attendant steam-launch and sailing-pinnace, but labour was cheap in these days, and it was appropriate that the president of a famous shipping company should own such a magnificent yacht. They did not go far afield, but spent the nights at anchor off Scalpay, and cruised among the long fiords of Ross-shire during the day. They had beautiful weather, and mother writes:

'Yesterday was bright and clear, with the bluest of seas and the bluest of skies. We left our moorings at breakfast time and sailed all day in and out of the grand lochs opposite Skye, Loch Torridon and Gair Loch. Imagine what it was like to sit under an awning in the best of company and glide among those glorious mountains, our only interruption being to go downstairs and partake of the choicest meals. Today the weather was not so gloriously fine, but the greyer sky suited the wild grandeur of Loch Hourn. We went as far as we could in the *Iolaire*, then all got into the little launch and steamed for about an hour longer far into the narrow upper loch. These places are not often seen, and we shall never see them under happier circumstances.'

Entertainment during the week was varied and interesting. 'One day we were at Armadale and called at the castle and saw the beautiful garden. Another day we spent on Scalpay; on another we went to Kyleakin and explored the old castle and had a jolly tea at the hotel. Every day Sir Donald had some delightful plan. He had a steam launch and a little sail-boat with red sails, so we were sometimes in one and sometimes in the other. If we happened to be becalmed when a meal-time was due, the little steam-launch came puffing along and towed us home'.

They came home after this refreshing carefree holiday feeling years younger, and carrying a little canary in a cage, a present from Sir Donald to the children. We were so thrilled by it that we had eyes for neither father nor mother, and I amused them by remarking that I was glad it was a canary and not a *vulture* that they had brought to us.

At last Nurse Chisholm left us. She had been invaluable in time of need, and had an expert hand with a baby, but sighs of relief were breathed at her departure. It is amusing that for the next few months mother continues to worry a little because Allan had not begun to speak. The child was not yet two, and was obviously intelligent: probably her elder children had been forward in their talking, which made her anxious about his more deliberate pace. Camas Bàn, the white bay, an uninhabited beach under Ben Tianavaig is the only stretch of sand near Portree; all the rest of the bay-shore is rock and shingle. On rare Saturday afternoons when the weather was fine and father free from work he would row us across with a picnic and a kettle. Mother would make a driftwood fire and scoop water in a cup from one of the runnels that seeped down from the moors above, through bog myrtle and butterwort and red rattle. We would run naked in sunshine and soft airs, splashing into the gently creaming sea, then all wet and shining, through the strap-leaves of the yellow irises to the sheep-bitten grass and the cold moss round a spring. Our feet tingled with the sensations of gritty sand, warm rock, rushes and bracken, and water welling between the toes. Portree village is out of sight behind the bay's western headland; there is an open view across the sea to Beal Point and the Ross-shire mountains rising behind Raasay. We felt as if we had landed on a desert island.

'Nurse left us last Monday, and we have been getting on splendidly without her. The noise of the nursery did not suit her, and I had the uncomfortable feeling that she was both critical and discontented. I did not know what was going on behind my back, and felt at sixes and sevens with my maids. After she left I had a talk with them and cleared the air, with the result that everything has gone smoothly and pleasantly this week. I have enjoyed having the baby more in my own hands, and Annie and I always work well together. The children don't seem to make so much noise now that there is no one to mind their din.

'Allan is not a bit further on with his speech, but his gestures are very amusing. Last week we took them for a picnic one afternoon in a boat over to Camus Bàn, the sandy bay opposite. They all had their clothes off and ran about naked on the sands, while their Daddy with long bare legs superintended the bathing operations. Now whenever Allan sees a boat the following pantomime goes on:- first vigorous pointings at the boat, then vigorous clappings of his own small body, which being interpreted means: — "Behold a boat! This man here was in a boat!" Then he points to each of us in turn with grunts to indicate who were his companions, and next he pulls at his clothes and tugs at his shoes to show what happened.

'Alasdair has invented a place called "Kennadi" and he and Isobel have long stories about it. He will sit for a long time quite still on a seat holding the end of a rope in the belief he is journeying to Kennadi. He and Isobel understand each other and live in a world of their own. You get glimpses into it when you hear scraps of conversation like this:

Isobel: 'Alasdair, will you lend me your stick for cutting off your monkeys' tails?'

Alasdair: 'No, I'm using it.'

"Where are your monkeys?" I asked. "Oh, they're in the Zoo at Kennadi".
— meantime he is vigorously working a small stick backwards and forwards in the sand'.

In April 1908 the Honourable Godfrey, second son of Lord Macdonald, had married, and two important social events that summer were a garden party given at the Lodge in Portree where the young couple were staying, and another at Armadale Castle in south Skye. This great golden-brown mansion now falling into ruin was built around 1820. It stands on a wooded hillside above the Sound of Sleat, a piece of mediæval artifice with towers, battlements, machiolations, arrow-slits and arched sash-windows; it is appropriate that the seat of the Lord of the Isles should owe so much to the novels of Sir Walter Scott. Some of the guests invited on these occasions showed a truly Highland disregard of time as one of the terms of an invitation.

'We had lots of strawberries and cream at the Lodge: everyone was invited, rich and poor, and all seemed to enjoy it. We were the last to go, as we had been detained in coming, and we left our host and hostess rather exhausted after their efforts, and ready to go in and rest. We were therefore amused to meet three country bodies some way from the gate, quietly making their way to the party, not realising that it was over or that time was any object. Of course they were received and duly entertained, but the man, who is three-quarters witted, was rather puzzled and not quite satisfied with what he described as "wee red things in milk"'.

Mother did not go to the Armadale party as Allan had had a slight accident, but father arrived at the castle in time for lunch with the family. "The party was to begin at four o'clock, so you can imagine their consternation when they were still at lunch, about two, to see a brake full of people arriving. They had come from Broadford and were making a day of it. The ladies fled to get ready, and Ronald and Mr. Godfrey took the people in hand and showed them views from distant parts of the estate till after three o'clock. I think Mrs Godfrey will be rather amused at our Skye way of keeping engagements'.

Towards the end of August Alasdair and I were taken to have a holiday with mother's family at Brodick, Isle of Arran: they had rented a house among the woods to the north of the village beside the Rosa burn where the jagged Goatfell ridge towers to the skyline. There was a great smooth crescent of golden sand to play on all day; the shore-background was briary and brambly, and we gathered luscious blackberries which did not grow around Portree.

The long slow journey from Portree to Glasgow could be made in a day; the boat left at seven a.m. in winter and eight in summer, and arrived at Mallaig towards mid-day. There the wonder began: we saw trains. The puffs of smoke among the heathery rocks and the hoots that echoed across the sound of Sleat enthralled us. Mallaig Station, glass-roofed with a trim of pierced and pointed wood, newly painted for the summer in buff and white and decorated with hanging baskets of lobelia and geraniums was the most exciting and romantic place imaginable. At last we were off, running along a single-track line between the hills and the sea, looking across the sands of Morar to the tilted anvil-shape of Eigg and the blue mountains of Rum, skirting the long sea-lochs, and stopping at every flower-decked station — Morar, Arisaig, Lochailort, Glenfinnan, Locheilside, Corpach — 'almost singing themselves they run'. At Fort William the line turned inland to make its way through scenery of wild grandeur, curving along the bases of mountains, crossing desolate moors and foaming rivers of dark amber, by Spean Bridge, Roy Bridge, Tulloch, Corrour, Rannoch, Bridge of Orchy, Tyndrum, and at last Crianlarich, the only station with a buffet where, in these pre-thermos days, passengers rushed to drink thick cups of scalding tea against time. Then we ran along Loch Lomond side, and crossed the ridge to Loch Long and Gareloch-head. When we reached Glasgow towards seven in the evening we were tired little teddy-bears, but not yet at our final destination. Inside the great arch of Queen Street station horse-drawn cabs were waiting: we clattered over the stone setts of Buchanan Street to Central or St Enoch's for the short journey to Paisley.

Going home was less exhausting as the train left Glasgow some time in mid-morning, and we spent a night at the West End Hotel, Fort William. We arrived in the dark and it generally seemed to be raining, but Miss MacIntosh our landlady was welcoming, and after a good night's sleep it was thrilling to waken in a strange place; to kneel with elbows on the windowsill and look at calm silver-grey Loch Linnhe with golden seaweed lying among the rocks, and a heron dipping its beak, and mist floating low on the mountains. We would catch the train in a leisurely way after breakfast and travel to Mallaig past lochans in the peat where water-lilies

Alasdair and Isobel in August 1908.

floated, and woods of birch and pine above the beaches of white sand. The boat was due in Portree around 5.20, but it often arrived later, since it had to connect at Kyle of Lochalsh with the Highland Railway train from Inverness which had very vague ideas of keeping to schedule, as two of the letters show. This description of homecoming in October is typical. My scorn of Portree was only the crossness of fatigue; I really loved the place.

'We all arrived safely last night after a comfortable journey. The children began to get very tired when it was after their bed-time; first Alasdair went to sleep on the seat, then Isobel on my knee. When we reached Fort William we had great difficulty in getting Alasdair wakened, and when he eventually did he *howled* and continued howling all the way to the hotel. There we were met by our kind landlady who carried him to our room and helped me to put him to bed. He howled steadily on through the process, but as soon as his head touched the pillow was fast asleep again. Isobel on the other hand took a lively interest in her surroundings, ate a good supper and went to bed, asking me to shut the door as she slept better in the dark. I thought she might feel nervous in a strange place, but she is too experienced a traveller for that.

'Next morning the children wakened us in good time, and we got away comfortably. We enjoyed the journey home, the sea part of it especially, as it was warm and calm. Isobel was not at all charmed with Portree when we reached it. "I don't like Portree at all. I've lived far too long in Portree". However when we really got home she was pleased. Allan was out at the door, and behind, Baby Flora in Annie's arms. Neither of them could express their sentiments in words, but they both expressed them all the same. Flora came to me at once, and chuckled to Isobel as if she knew her, and Allan danced about, gurgling and laughing. He was greatly pleased to have us home again, and trots after Alasdair in little brotherly fashion'.

Isobel with baby Flora, Allan and Alasdair.

When a ship of the Royal Navy came into Portree Bay and lay at anchor, grey and majestic, in the deep water between the Black Rock and Ben Tianavaig it enlivened the whole community, and even strict Sabbatarians could not resist the temptation to go visiting on a Sunday night.

'We are having an exciting time in Portree. The *King Edward*, the flagship of the Home Fleet has been in the bay for the last few days with around 900 men on board. It is a great sight to see the blue-jackets landing and, headed by a magnificent brass band, marching up to the parade-ground behind the village. So long as they are there, there is not much chance of steady work either for mistresses or for maids, with sailors always in sight, men signalling with flags, bugles blowing, and a good deal of rowdiness and larking. When I looked out this morning the first thing I saw was two huge bread-baskets hoisted to the top of the Royal Hotel flagpole. I have just had an application from Lexy to allow her and Annie to go out and see through the ship. I am amused to find that their Sabbatarian principles can be a little elastic at times. Not so long ago one of them refused to carry a parcel up to Miss Maclachlan's on a Sunday night'.

Then came the adventure of a tea-party on board the *King Edward*. We were lifted into a steam-launch with a shining brass funnel and a crew of cheerful weather-tanned sailors: it sped across the grey water, crashing into waves with its bow. I remember the magnificent box of chocolates bright with coloured foil in the centre of the ward-room table under the hanging lamp. Mr. Gillanders was the big kindly headmaster of Portree School, and the two Mackinnon children, Neil and Peggy, were near our age.

'On Monday one of the officers of the *King Edward VII* asked Ronald and me and the two older children to come out and have tea on board. Mrs Mackinnon and her two bairns were there too, and Mr. Gillanders. We had a great time of it; he was so kind, and you should have seen him hauling the four babies, for they were nothing else — Isobel was the oldest — up and down the steep stairs. They were greatly delighted, and the whys went whizzing round like bullets. After we had seen round we went to the ward-room for tea. I was afraid one of the babies would disgrace us by spilling its tea, but everything passed off well. Beside the usual cake there was a fine box of chocolates which added to the success of the meal'.

At the beginning of November our garden was still full of flowers in the mild autumn weather of the west Highlands, Wearing our butcher-blue overalls we played in the sand which our gardener had brought over in sacks from Camas Bàn, or had climbing lessons from father among the rocks.

'This is the first day of winter according to the calendar, but I have just come in from the garden with specimens of forty-four different flowers in my hand. We haven't had a touch of frost so far, so not only have we a great variety, but showy flowers like chrysanthemums and dahlias are blooming in great luxuriance. The children are all blooming as vigorously as the other flowers. Alasdair has got an old wheel rigged up on the garden-seat for a steering-wheel, and they all sail away in his boat to enchanted lands of their own. Daddy has been taking the three of them up the Lump for climbing exercises. They all enjoy it, even wee Allan who makes brave attempts and then calls piteously for "Daddy! Daddy!" to lift him down. Last Saturday we took the two eldest for a long walk up by the reservoir. They had a fine scamper over the moors, but I think it was far enough for Alasdair, for when tea was ready he did not come, and we found him fast asleep, curled up in a big chair'.

The great event of the autumn was the wedding of Miss Emily Pauline Macleod, eldest daughter of Norman Magnus, the 26th Chief of Macleod, to Captain Nicol Martin of Glendale in Skye. It took place in the beautiful drawing-room of Dunvegan Castle, once the great hall of the mediæval keep, now elegant with marble mantelpiece, crystal chandeliers and grand piano, the only sign of its great age being the depth of the window embrasures which look west over Loch Dunvegan to strange-shaped rocky islets and the hills of Harris. Here Doctor Johnson, storm-stayed for eleven days, had enjoyed more civilised company and intelligent conversation than he had found in Armadale or Raasay; his portrait hangs on the wall and near it his framed letter of thanks, written in a firm masculine hand of great character. There is also a letter from Walter Scott, not yet a baronet, acknowledging hospitality received in 1814 when he was gathering material for *The Lord of the Isles*. Mother writes on October 25th:-

'We have hired the motor belonging to the Broadford hotel to take us over, so we shall not need to spend the night. There is an alarming report that it is to be a teetotal wedding, a thing unknown in the Highlands, and not at all approved of'. It was: and that extraordinary departure from custom is still remembered in Skye.

So on Thursday the 29th they set out at ten o'clock in the morning with Sheriff Campbell and Louie Fraser, sister of father's partner, in one of those high-built open vehicles so unsuitable to the Skye climate. One can imagine the dust-coats and capes, the mushroom hats and sporting caps and motor-veils as the car snorted off for the drive by moors and sea-lochs to Dunvegan.

'We took our wedding finery in boxes, so we had a considerable amount of luggage between us, and looked as if we were going off for a month at least. We had the most delightful run to Dunvegan; it was not at all cold and we were all in high spirits. We arrived there between twelve and one, and found brave attempts to make the village look as gay as possible; dimunitive flags tied here and there to the rudimentary chimneys of crofting huts, and more ambitious efforts by those who had superior residences. We exchanged greetings with our fellow-guests at the hotel and went to our rooms to dress, then we joined the other kilts and white waistcoats and flowers and furbelows, and sat down to a very meagre lunch, not at all in keeping with the imposing appearance of the company. When we were half through we heard the rousing tones of the pipes, and made a rush to the door to see the bridegroom being conveyed in solemn procession to the castle. First came the band in Highland dress with pipes and drum, then about thirty Lovat Scouts on horseback, two abreast. Then came the carriage in which sat two gorgeous but most unhappy-looking men in full Highland dress with tartan plaid on shoulder. One was the bridegroom, Mr Nicol Martin, the other was our friend Major Macdonald of Flodigarry who was best man. They greeted us with as cheerful a smile as they could command, and passed slowly on, followed by another score of Scouts on horseback.

'The castle is about a mile from the hotel. Louie and I got the chance of a drive up, and the others walked. When we got there we found the Scouts and their horses grouped picturesquely about the castle yard. We were met by Macleod who greeted us in his own kind, homely fashion, then we went to the drawing-room where the ceremony was to be performed. There were not very many guests, so we had not the feeling of being lost in a crowd, and I knew a good many of them, so felt quite at home.

'Soon "The voice that breathed o'er Eden" struck up, and the bridal procession came in. The bride looked very well in her robes, as she is tall and dark, and was quite happy and composed. The two bridesmaids were also in white, with small green wreaths on their hair and girdles of Macleod tartan round their waists and caught up at the side. The service was the Church of England one, so the two clergymen in their white surplices and the bridegroom and best man in their bright tartans made a very picturesque group, especially in its setting in one of the oldest rooms of the castle. The sun came through one of the deep-set windows and fell on the bride, which was pretty as well as a good omen. Just beside me was the case containing the Fairy Flag and other interesting historical relics. Both bride and bridegroom were quite cool, and repeated the long responses which the English service demands clearly and unfalteringly.

'After the service there were the usual congratulations and laughter and talk, then we all went out and were photographed in front of the castle. Then two interesting presentations were made. The Scouts assembled in the drawing-room and presented their captain, Mr. Nicol Martin, with a handsome silver tray, and afterwards in the library, Mr. Cameron of Gesto presented Mrs Martin with a piano and pianola from the tenantry. Then we went to the dining-room for tea. The bride cut the cake, and we were all very merry without feeling the want of any stronger stimulant. While we were at tea the bride disappeared to change, then we all went out to wait for the departure.

'The send-off was almost the prettiest part of the day. The Scouts formed a double line from the door down the avenue to where a motor-car was waiting. At the word of command they crossed bayonets, forming a line of arches, the band struck up, and the bride and bridegroom passed under it, assailed by the usual shower of rice and confetti, to the skirling of the pipes. After that we walked back to the hotel, changed and had a delightful run home in the soft evening air'.

During the first week of November father was in Broadford for three days on Crofter Commission business. The affairs at Elgol and Strathaird with which he was then concerned, and the later cases of the Valtersay squatters and the rebellion against the Congested Districts Board at Idrigill near Uig are pieces of Highland history, with which he was closely connected. Allan's slowness to speak was still causing some anxiety but his pleasure in attractive and becoming clothes was a characteristic that appeared early — he was still under two years old. In this he was very different from his brother who never cared much about dress.

'I don't know when Allan is going to learn to speak, but in spite of his want of language he enters into all the other children's games and makes himself understood. He amuses us at present by a passion he has for a certain blue smock embroidered in white. He weeps tears of rage if he has to put on any other dress, and if he catches a glimpse of this one in his drawer it is no use trying to induce him to put on another. One day he made the great discovery of it in the dirty-clothes basket: he dragged it triumphantly into the nursery and tried to put it on on top of the one he was wearing. It happens to be the dress he looks best in, and he seems to be quite aware of the fact.'

Later in the month Alasdair, now aged three, was beginning to speculate. 'Alasdair's mind has been taken up with his origin this week. "Did God make me out of a dog?" seems to suggest a glimmering of the theory of the transmigration of souls. "Where did you put my wings when I came?" was another of his questions. He would not have been surprised if I had taken them out of a drawer, carefully rolled up in tissue paper. "Who made Mama?" was another query. "O, God made Mama", "And did she come straight from the sky down to the garden?"'

During November a severe epidemic of measles was spreading in the village; one little girl had died of it. Neither Annie nor Lexy had had the illness, and mother was a little worried, as she could not keep them from contact with their friends in the neighbourhood. But life went on: poor Flora had an alarming experience, and Alasdair continued to speculate.

'We have had a new table made for the nursery and covered with white oilcloth, where the children can have their meals comfortably, and can sit at it and paint or string beads. It was rather high when it came, so I sent for the joiner to shorten it. Poor Baby was all alone in the nursery when he arrived, and when the door opened and a great bearded man clad in apron and shirt-sleeves and holding a large saw entered, her terror knew no bounds. She screamed with all her might, and Annie and I had to rush to comfort her.

'Alasdair is still pursuing his enquiries into the origin of things. "How does God make dogs? Does he put in their bones at their mouths?" being one of his questions. They are well so far, though I can hardly wipe their noses without feeling apprehension'.

But in mid-December trouble began: Lexy woke up one morning covered in spots. 'Don't you think it is a little inconsiderate for a *cook* to take measles in Christmas week, especially when she had already taken whooping-cough this year and had her wages raised?' mother asks ruefully. The children had been kept in a good deal by bad weather, and they invented a rather sinister game.

'The children have been very good in the house and play by themselves when we are all busy. I sent them down to the nursery while I got some writing done, and later I went down to see them. Isobel seemed alone. "Where's Alasdair?" I asked. "There", she said, pointing to a crumpled heap under a flannel apron. "He's in his grave. I'm playing at a graveyard, and these are the graves". Various toy animals were doing duty for the other occupants, covered by an assortment of garments, while her Daddy's boot-trees were gravestones at the head of each. All the time I was in the nursery Alasdair neither moved nor spoke, so he was entering into the spirit of the game, or perhaps he didn't dare'.

There followed a very strenuous Christmas and New Year. The aunt who lived with Catriona Cameron had a stroke, and mother spent two nights sitting with her, as it was difficult to get nursing help. She came home from one of her vigils to find Annie in bed with a severe attack of measles, and had to nurse her and look after the children. Fortunately none of them caught the infection, though they had been in close contact with Annie during her incubation period. It would have been a serious matter if poor Flora had had to go through both whooping-cough and measles before she was one year old.

1909: 'What A Lot They Have To Learn!'

In the opening letters of 1909 the troubles of living on a distant island are vividly described: serious illness in two houses, with the doctor laid low and the nurse and chemist on holiday. But mother takes it all in her stride.

'Annie, I am glad to say, has got the turn. She has had a very sharp attack, much worse than Lexy's. For two days her eyes were quite closed and her temperature over 104, so I felt a little anxious, especially as the doctor has not been well this week and the nurse is away, so that I could get no professional advice at all, but had to rely on myself and Black's Medical Dictionary. This has been a sad place for anyone anxious about sick friends; the nurse and chemist were both away for holidays, and the doctor was supposed to keep the chemist's shop going, so when he took ill we could not even get a dose of medicine. Catriona has had a most anxious week with poor Auntie, and has not even had a servant to help her. She got an old woman, but she was not very efficient, and a few days ago she announced she was "fair done" and went off. It is hard to have a serious illness in the house and have neither proper help nor professional advice'.

Dr Dewar's illness was more serious than had been thought at first, and in the third week of January he died. The funeral procession to the pier through rain-washed streets lit by scattered oil-lamps must have been an impressive sight. He was to be buried in Easdale on Scil Island, so the coffin would have a complicated journey by Mallaig and Oban.

'We have all been greatly grieved over the death of Dr Dewar, who seemed such a strong healthy man. He was to be buried in Easdale, so the Portree part of the funeral was between six and seven in the morning, before the boat started. A wild and wintry morning it was, and a weird scene it must have been, the large company in the dark on the pier as the boat slowly made off. Ronald had to go in all his Free Mason rig-out; he came back soaking, with feet like ice and a ruined tall hat'.

Problems were raised by the Sabbatarian principles of the attendants engaged by Catriona to help nurse her aunt. For some reason making or mending a fire on Sunday was considered a particularly heinous sin by the stricter Presbyterians.

'Miss Maclauchlan is making good progress. The nurse left yesterday, and we have got what we hope will be a suitable woman. She is strong and kindly, but has never been used to anything but country work, so she has a good deal to learn. To show you the difficulties we have to contend with, she was quite shocked today when Catriona asked her to tidy Auntie's fire and take the ashes away. She did it reluctantly, and explained that she had always been brought up to keep the Sabbath; she would do any work for Miss Cameron during the week, but she must not ask her to work on Sunday. I think she would have liked to go to church all day, but Catriona explained that the other girl had to go at night, so she could only go in the morning. The old woman we got in at first insisted on going twice to church, which meant that she would be out almost the whole day, although Miss Maclauchlan was so ill that we did not know if she would get through the day, and when Tuesday came she must get out to the prayer-meeting. So you see we are godly folks up here!'

Annie and Lexy recovered, and the children continued to thrive. Allan was slowly learning to speak, and the baby, not yet one, was catching up with him.

'Allan is trying every word now, but it is a foreign language to most folk, and a good deal of it even to me. His name for Baby is "Ni-nin-che-che"; what he means by it I have no idea. I generally take an apple to the nursery after lunch and divide it among the children. Today I went without it, and the wee ball on the floor looked up and said expectantly, "Ap-pa?" I am sorry you are missing so much of her. She is so sweet to hug these cold days".

On Saturday afternoons when father was free from the bank and the office we were taken for delightful rambles by the shore. 'Yesterday we had our Saturday ramble to the Black Rock and hunted for crabs and fishes in little pools. Isobel managed to catch a fish, but they would wriggle out of Alasdair's fat fingers. He was more successful with crabs, but unfortunately they "stuck their fingers into my flesh" as he expressed it, which caused howls. They had their usual climbing exercises under Daddy's supervision, and then trotted home at our heels'. On another occasion poor Alasdair asked Daddy to find him a *kind* crab. 'Those he had found for himself had not been kind'.

She goes on to illustrate the problem of unshaken faith and the dangers of rash prayer. 'What is troubling Isobel at present is that in an unguarded moment she asked God to send an ogre, the reason being that she wanted to see what one was like. Now, however, fear has got the better of curiosity, and she is afraid her request will be granted. Whenever there is an unaccountable noise among the pipes in the bathroom or elsewhere, she says in an awestruck voice, "What's that? Perhaps it's the ogre coming!" — Alasdair's comment being, "Well, you shouldn't have asked for it, Isobel"'.

In February the United Free Church decided to have a Soirée, and mother as a prominent member of the congregation helped to organise it. This kind of social gathering, pronouce Swarree, used to liven the dreariness of winter in Scottish villages. Tea was brewed, and 'pokes' — paper bags of baker's food — were handed round: they usually contained, among other things, a currant slice or 'fly sandwich', a parkin biscuit made with treacle and oatmeal, and a raised bun dotted with preserving sugar. The orange given on the way out would help to counteract the starchiness of the fare. The entertainment was what the minister thought suitable and what local talent could provide. Mr. Macleod the U.F. minister was a white-bearded bachelor in poor health with no interest in sociability, so the swarree must have been suggested by the more enterprising of the congregation. The children mentioned were not mother's own family who were too young for such festivities, but the junior members of the church.

'The next thing we have to do is to get up a congregational Soirée. We haven't had such a thing for the last seventeen years, so we are not beyond the need of it. It is to come off on Friday week, and I am on the committee. It is not a very easy task to accomplish, as the tea will have to be made in Mrs Munro's kitchen and carried over. There is to be a magic lantern, speeches, and a little sacred music by the choir, so we are not likely to get too hilarious. We will have pokes at the door and an orange going out in the good old style. One of our difficulties is that we have five merchants in the church who must have equal shares in our patronage for tea, sugar, fruit etc. So we shall have to walk warily, giving offence to none'.

And two weeks later. 'Our Soirée is now a thing of the past, and I am glad to say it got on very well. We had a full church, and I felt rather anxious, as it is not easy to make tea for a churchful of folks with one small urn and an army of black kettles on a kitchen range at a considerable distance from the scene of operations, and have it carried on a cold night across the Square, kettle by kettle. But we did manage it, and the tea was both good and hot. It might be expected when there is only one Soirée in seventeen years that the folk would want good measure, so we had a long long programme that had to be curtailed to let us out before eleven. The choir sang some hymns which are as good as anthems up here where we hear nothing but psalms, and the children also sang. Then there was a magic lantern which was manipulated by Mr. Munro. But as he is the most nervous man imaginable, and as they had only a short time to show some 67 slides, the effect was more like the northern lights than anything else, especially as they were rather out of focus. However the children seemed quite pleased, and if the slides appeared upside down as often as any other way, that only added to their enjoyment. The subject was 'Scenes from Palestine', and as they were a little dim it didn't matter *very* much that at times Mr. Munro was four or five slides ahead of Mr. Gillanders who was trying to explain them. Every now and then a slide came on that was obviously wrong, then they found out where they were and started fair again. However, these are trifles when they are met in the right spirit!'

But the stricter sect in the adjoining Free Presbyterian church deplored such frivolities, and their minister preached a sermon against 'those who in unseemly fashion were eating and drinking in the House of God, and singing hymns'. Another thing was troubling them; the village now had the convenience of a milk-cart which delivered supplies at the doors and saved everyone from having to call daily at the Home Farm. But it delivered on the Sabbath, and some people even paid for their milk on that sacred day, which the Seceders found very shocking.

By this time I was five years old, and should have gone to school, but mother thought it would be too tiring, and taught me at home. I learned to read easily, and developed an early taste for the lurid and sensational.

'Isobel is now trying to make out stories for herself. She got hold of a magazine in which there was a gruesome story about a certain Alec, and was greatly interested in it, as far as she could make it out. "Oh, here's something more about Alec!" she would cry, and then read, "No, Alec, I will not forgive you. I will forgive the girl, but you must die like the dog you are!" — then a little later — "Here's more about Alec! 'Where is Alec?' asked the girl. At that moment the dead face of Alec appeared in the net, and the next it was drawn down, down, down!" I thought it wiser to have the magazine disappear as well as Alec'.

But a Saturday walk by the Scorrybreck burn on the last day of February brought the greatest delight. It flowed through the Lodge grounds, with silvery branches of hazel dipping to the brown water, and great clumps of rhododendron waiting to flower in purple, ivory and rose later in the year.

'How Isobel enjoyed our walk yesterday afternoon! As soon as we got out she exclaimed, "Oh what a delightful salt smell of the sea! I'm *so* glad I was born on an island with sea all round it!" We went up the burn beside the Lodge, and all the time she was rejoicing in the rippling of the water and the green of the moss. But the culmination of it all was when she found what must be the very first primrose of the year. A primrose by the river's brim is something more than a yellow primrose to our wee lass'.

At the beginning of March we had some wild weather ending in a snow-storm. Father had gone to stay with Mr. Thomson of Strathaird in his shooting-lodge at Camusunary on Loch Scavaig. This is one of the wildest parts of Skye: to reach it he had to drive to Sligachan, then ride through the Cuillins on a pony. He started out in the fine weather at the end of February, on a Sunday: then he was snowed up, and nothing was heard of him till Thursday when mother had a telegram saying he would arrive that night. I arranged the sofa with cushions and a rug, thinking he would be in a state of exhaustion. During the same week mother served at a soup-kitchen which had been started to help the poorer people of the district. It seems to have been needed. 'I was surprised to see how far some of the folks came for soup. We had three from Woodend, two and a half miles through a wild snowstorm for a can of broth, and all the way back again. Some of them were well over seventy'.

Our education continued happily. 'Alasdair is great on sewing, though his fat fingers need much guidance, and Isobel is finding her way out of lesson books to real books. She can read *The Cat that Walked by Himself* without the least trouble; she has heard it read pretty often, but she makes good attempts at other *Just So Stories* she has never heard before. A queer jumble a child's mind is too! "Wouldn't it be funny", she said to me the other day, "if Jesus went into a room in the sky and found the sun lying

48

asleep with all its rays stuck out and a smile on its face?" There is a good deal that needs to be put right there!"

In April Lexy decided to leave us, mother remarking, 'She has not been very satisfactory of late, not to mention her disposition to catch any infection that is going'. All through April and May the spring-cleaning went on: twelve rooms, some of them very large, as well as stair-cases and passages had to be thoroughly cleansed from the grime produced by a winter of coal fires and oil lamps. Annie and Bella shared in the work, and the children had to look after themselves.

'The children have invented a new game this week. They have been turned loose to play while we are all busy spring-cleaning, and have discovered some dirty waste ground between us and the pier-road which is the resort of all the hens in the neighbourhood. I found them squatted in different parts of it and asked them what they were doing. "We're hens, and sitting on our nests". This unattractive place is a perfect paradise to them, and they are off like a shot to it as soon as they get out. Another day I looked over the wall and could see only Isobel and Allan. "What are you doing now?" I called. "We're playing at house". "And where is Alasdair?" "He's down the road looking for lions". "Has he found any?" "Yes". "And what does he do with them?" "Oh, he drags them up by the neck and we burn them on the fire, and they cook our supper for us". And sure enough there was a mild-looking laddie in a blue overall mixing with the wayfarers on the road who, I'm afraid, failed to recognise in him the mighty hunter of lions'.

In June we had a meeting with a notable Highlander, Father John Macmillan, who was born in Barra, and was parish priest in Eigg and later at Northbay in his native island. He had a wide knowledge of Gaelic tradition and folklore, and published in 1929 a collection of Hebridean songs recalled from his childhood or gathered from his parishoners. Father and he had many interests in common. I remember how he appeared on that summer evening, wearing a coat with capes and a wide black clerical hat, and how we knew him at once as a man who loved children, even before he took our hands and led us up the village street for this wonderful largesse of toys. Alasdair wanted to fire his new gun, but I was afraid of the noise, so Father John held me gently with a hand over each of my ears in a comfortable and sympathetic way while Alasdair enjoyed himself with percussion caps.

'The children had a great adventure the other day. Daddy was giving Alasdair and Isobel rides on his new bicycle in front of the house when a gentleman came up who was introduced to me as Father John Macmillan, a Catholic priest whom Ronald had met in Eigg. He made great friends with the children, then said, "Come with me and get some chocolate". So off they went, hatless and untidy as they were, and were gone a long time. When they returned they were wild with excitement. He gave them a box of chocolates each, then he bought Alasdair a gun and Isobel a beautiful doll. I felt quite ashamed to see him when he called later in the evening".

Early in August our Highland grandmother came from Glenhinisdale for the Communion services during which enough prayer and fasting went on to exorcise a legion of evil spirits.

'This has been our Communion Sunday — always a busy and upsetting day with me. As Isobel feelingly remarked, "This is a very funny kind of Sunday!" She did not at all approve of it for they had neither dinner nor tea with us, and the usual order of the day was quite upset. Grannie has been with us since Wednesday, and her services are neither short nor few. My heart is sore for poor old Grannie who comes back from these senselessly long services exhausted and faint from want of food. It makes me angry to see an old body like that going from nine in the morning till nearly five in the afternoon without a bite, and sitting on a hard seat till her back is nearly broken. All I can do is to get her off to bed to lie down as soon as she has had some food, and then she is hardly settled before she is up for the next service. I really can't say I enjoy her visits, though I like her so much herself'.

Later Alasdair and I were taken for a holiday to Lossiemouth, a fishing village and golfing resort in Morayshire. We travelled by Inverness to the east coast of Scotland where sandy beaches stretch by links and dunes to a distant lighthouse. The air was bracing; the light clearer and harder than in the western isles, and I found different wild flowers, also of clear bright colours: yellow bedstraw, scarlet poppies and blue harebells. Mother was teaching me to know wild flowers by making a list of their names every year as I found them; she wrote it for me till I could write myself, and there was a reward of sixpence when I reached a hundred, and another sixpence for a hundred and twenty. So it was interesting to find some that did not grow in Skye, especially when they had beautiful names, like the rest-harrow that crept among the grass on the sandy wastes near the sea, or the aromatic yellow buttons of tansy. We dictated letters to Grannie one wet afternoon; there had been a visit to Elgin where we met history in the ruins of the mediæval cathedral, burned down out of spite by the Wolf of Badenoch. 'We saw the big cathedral, and it was awfully big, and a man burned it down'. There was also a circus, which must have been a magnificent spectacle as described by Alasdair.

'I saw a clown that bumped over little boys, and they couldn't do it very well so he had to give them a kick, and I saw a naked man on a swing. There were dear old men on horses, and a horse that spit out flames and fire. And the horses went running round with men standing on them, and there was a big elephant was so awful big and a big trunk on it and it ate up people whenever it wanted. And there was a funny horse made up of two men and the clown gave it a kick and one man fell out'. Alasdair also went to church for the first time at the age of four, and was disconcerted as children are when they first find themselves experiencing pain or tedium from which there is no escape.

'I took Alasdair to church today for the first time. He was very restless, and when I whispered to him to be quiet he would answer "But I'm not very comfortable!" During the prayers he lay along the seat on his tummy, and had various other attitudes during the sermon'. But none-the-less he was a religious little boy. 'Alasdair was puzzling his head the other day about where all the sand came from. His Daddy tried to give him a scientific explanation, but he cut him short with his own simpler one. "I suppose Jesus has lots of *malts* in the sky and he just pours them down on this place." A malt is their name for a bag, from a picture in one of their books of "the malt that lay in the house that Jack built", and as their own garden-sand arrives in bags from Camas Bàn it was natural to suppose that the sand here came in the same way. Jesus is a great personage in this scheme of things. "Why do trains go on rails? I suppose Jesus had a plan that way, but he had another plan for tar-engines in towns, for they don't go on rails."'

In October an inconvenient responsibility was casually imposed on us by Mr. John Macdonald, the brother of father's benefactor and something of a grandee, who was going south for winter. Redcliffe is a beautiful old stone mansion with well-proportioned oriel and sash windows that look out to sea over a low-walled terrace garden above the shore. George Fraser was father's partner, and Willie was our gardener Willie Ross.

'The Redcliffe Macdonalds left this week. On the morning of their departure Ronald got a note from Mr. John saying he was rather worried about his pictures which are very valuable, and suggesting that Ronald and Mr. Fraser might take five of them and hang them in their public rooms until he came back. George Fraser refused to have anything to do with them, so, as Ronald could not afford to disoblige his client, there was nothing for it but to take the whole of them himself. I really did not know whether to be more amused or angry when they arrived — five *immense* pictures, three of them family portraits. Fancy imagining that anyone in an ordinary house has space to hang five huge pictures — one of them I am sure is six feet high! Not only that, but they are very valuable, and are insured, I believe, for £1,000. Two of them are by Poynter, a huge one of *The Prodigal Son* and a portrait of Mrs Macdonald's father. There they were, dumped in the dining-room, and the next thing was where to put them, and how to get them hung. Meantime I was in terror that Alasdair might put a stick through them or injure them in some way. It was a day or two before we could get the joiner to come, and then he and I and Willie between us managed with many groans and sighs to get them all hung in the dining-room. All our own pictures had to be taken down, and three of them now adorn the nursery. We hardly know ourselves now in our own dining-room. Opposite the door we have *The Prodigal Son*, and over the mantelpiece *The Exiled Jacobite* by Lidderdale. We have got a good deal of fun out of it as well as considerable worry. In future Ronald is to remember that the lady with the very low dress and handsome shoulders is his mother-in-law. Old Harry Macdonald is his father, and the beautiful Poynter I claim as an ancestor of my own.'

I was well away with my reading by then, and Allan was also developing. 'Isobel is greatly taken with the *Song of Hiawatha* at present; she manages the long words wonderfully, but she sometimes makes funny mistakes. She told me that she had read such a nice story in a magazine. It was called *The Little White Slave* and was about a doom-stick servant — not, after all, a very far-fetched rendering of "domestic".

'Allan, seated on the sofa-arm, was asking me the other day if "War" was a place. "I am riding to war, you know, and that chair over there is War." What a lot they have to learn!'

Church-going in November was a dismal experience which the children did not yet have to endure. But Alasdair, still in religious mood, tried to conduct a service from the dangerous and slippery height of the whorled mahogany pillar that ended the red stairs' bannister.

'I wish we could get a new stove in church. Today there were very few there, and I think everyone except me, but including the minister, had a cold. The one inefficient stove was smoking, further to irritate the vocal chords of the congregation. I am afraid we were a little hypocritical when we sang, "I joyed when to the House of God, Go up they said to me", and one felt that to re-write the line to "Jerusalem, within thy gates, My feet shall *frozen* be," might not be far from the truth.

'I got rather a fright with Alasdair today. After we had left, the family took it into its head to play at church in the downstairs lobby. Alasdair as minister perched himself on the end of the bannisters, and in the fervour of his exhortations overbalanced and landed on his head. When I got home I found him asleep in bed and looking very white. He couldn't take any dinner and was limp all day, but by the evening he was up and quite jolly again, and ready for a good tea. He has a nasty bruise on his forehead, but otherwise is none the worse.

'Some of his remarks are not very easy to answer. What would you say if this was addressed to you in a cheery tone? — "Mama, if Daddy died we would have Jesus for our Father, and *wouldn't that be nice!*" He brought me a biscuit the other day and asked what was written on it. I replied that it was "Rich Tea" and the name of the man that made it. "Is it Jesus that's written on it?" he asked reverently. "No, it's McVitie and Price", I replied.'

Late in November father motored to Dunvegan and crossed the Minch to Lochmaddy in North Uist where he defended the position of the Congested Districts Board in the affair of the Vatersay squatters. It was a long journey and he had to go again early in December, but the sea was reasonably calm for both crossings. While he was away Alasdair and I were taken to tea at the Lodge which Lady Macdonald had let to a Captain and Mrs Money who had a boy and girl near our ages. The nursery full of exotic toys and food, and the walk home by night, made a great adventure in our quiet lives.

'We were invited to the Lodge, the children to tea in the nursery, and I to tea downstairs. They did enjoy themselves! There was a rocking-horse and lots of beautiful toys; there were apples and prunes and chocolate for tea as well as sponge-cake, and last of all they walked home in the dark night with the moonlight and starlight, a thing they had never done before, and saw the magic lights of the boats at the pier, and the familiar burn looking weird and unfamiliar in the moonlight. Isobel in her queer way expressed her feelings by quoting:-

"There was no light in earth or heaven
But the cold light of stars".

I did not recognise the quotation, but she said it came from her book of Longfellow's poems'.

Towards the middle of December the canary which Sir Donald Currie had given us and which hung in its cage by the west window of the library came to a sad end. One morning when mother went to give it seed and water she found a mutilated mass of feathers on the cage floor, and thought that a mouse must have run up the curtains and killed it.

'Partly because I could not bring myself to speak of it, and partly to spare their feelings I did not tell the children, but waited till they noticed it. Would you believe it? — not one of the little wretches has missed their canary! On Thursday night Isobel was drawing a bird; Alasdair asked her what it was, and she drew aside the curtains to show him. She had just said, "The bird's not there!" when they upset Daddy's tobacco-jar, which turned the current of their thoughts, and since then they have not said a word about it. Alasdair said something about its perhaps being in the drawing-room when Isobel missed it, so they may think it is there'.

But our reactions when at last we found out what had happened made an interesting piece of child psychology; in one day we passed from acute sensibility to cheerful callousness.

'They discovered the loss of the bird at last, and there was much weeping and wailing, especially from Isobel. Alasdair took the thing more philosophically, and suggested to comfort her that we might get another bird. "Yes, but it might be a *rook!*" she sobbed, the bare thought of which opened the flood-gates afresh. She amused me by holding her hands over her ears one minute and saying, "Don't tell me about it, Mama, please don't tell me! — it's far too sad!" and then asking questions to bring out more ghastly details. But the end of it was that on the very same day the whole tragedy was converted into a grand game played with much noise and fun. Allan would be the bird, perched on the garret stairs; Alasdair, the mouse, would creep up and go for him. Isobel would act the Mama and go up with a glass of water and discover the disaster. Then they would change parts and go over the whole thing again'.

We were now old enough to enjoy Christmas, and there was no measles to spoil everything as there had been the year before. Willie the gardener made me a doll's house out of an orange-box, and Santa Claus arrived in style.

'You may be sure they were early afoot on Christmas morning, and wildly excited over the stockings which contained an apple, a tangerine orange, a banana, a few raisins and sweets, a penny packet of chocolate, some handkerchiefs, a twopenny toy and a penny in the toe. Then at the foot of the bed the furniture, the motor-car and the soldier's outfit, enough to turn any child's head. I was nearly deafened when I arrived on the scene; even wee Flora, whose little white stocking couldn't hold very much, was chuckling loudly over her dolly. They did not realise that anything more was coming, so when we came up from breakfast and found the piano nearly covered with parcels and toys there were scenes of great excitement. Allan was delighted to get an outfit like Alasdair's, and very charming the two wee boys looked with the scarlet over their blue jerseys'.

There had been some severe frost and snow during that December when the mid-winter General Election of 1909-1910 was taking place, and when father, who was strongly attached to the Conservative cause had been helping in the campaign. He had toured the island with Sir Reginald Macleod's agent, making speeches in Gaelic and English, and enduring a good deal of hardship in spite of an up-to-date Christmas present.

'Ronald and I gave each other a handsome present this year, namely a thermos flask and case. We have already found it useful, for Ronald had to go down the country to collects rents on Friday. It was bitterly cold, and he had to stay all day in a house where there had been no fire since he was there a year ago, and where there was no glass in the windows. He took the thermos flask with him and had some hot coffee in the middle of the day. Poor Ronald has had a very hard week of it: cold weather and early starts and much exposure, sometimes speaking in the open air. I daresay you will think that they would have been better at home than trying to forward the Unionist cause, but you see, Ronald thinks differently. He was so tired when he came home that he slept on the sofa most of Christmas day'.

We can form a picture of this election during which father worked so hard, from the history books and from the *Inverness Courier*. The Liberal government of 1906-1909 has passed the Old Age Pensions Act, to take effect from January 1909. This grant of 5/- a week at the age of seventy was like a gift from heaven to aged crofters who had never in the whole course of their lives handled much money, and would certainly not have been able to save any. To cover the expense of the pensions and of strengthening the navy to meet German threats Lloyd George in his 1909 Budget increased the death duties and the taxes on tobacco and liquor, raised income tax from 1/- to 1/2d in the £ and introduced super-tax in a very small way on incomes above £3,000. These measures were violently opposed by the Conservatives, and after being passed by the Commons the budget was rejected by the House of Lords in November 1909. A General Election followed.

Scotland had always been predominantly Liberal, and in this particular election the Conservatives appeared as grasping rich men who grudged the small contribution exacted from them to provide some relief for the aged poor. Nevertheless, when Sir Reginald Macleod K.C.B., brother of Norman Magnus, the 26th Chief, decided to contest Inverness-shire for the

Unionists, he was a strong candidate because of his historic name and the tradition of clan loyalty, even though Sir John Dewar, the sitting Liberal member, was a very able man who took a keen interest in Highland affairs. Between the dissolution of Parliament in November and the polling-day in January the weather was appalling, but both candidates toured their enormous constituency with heroic determination. Sir Reginald held fifty-six meetings on the mainland, then crossed to the Outer Isles early in the year, where he visited Barra, Eriskay and South Uist, and crossed the North Ford by horse and trap in a hurricane. On January 21st he was in Skye, holding meetings at Sconser, Braes, Raasay and Portree. But Sir John Dewar had been there before him, and the Liberal cause had been ably assisted by J. G. Mackay, the Portree hardware merchant, a local character of strong convictions and a dramatic turn of oratory. 'What have the Tories done for the Highlands and Islands?' he demanded on a later occasion. 'They have provided piers which are unapproachable by land and sea, and they have protected the St. Kilda wren.' This forceful speaker had been saying that if the Conservatives were returned every slated house would have a tax of 10/- put on it, and the price of oatmeal would be more than doubled. Sir Reginald laughed at these dismal prophecies; he promised to have a pier or slip built at Braes and to support a reduction of rates; he held a meeting in the cabin of the *Glencoe* on the way to Kyleakin 'with the permission of Captain Baxter the genial skipper', but all in vain. The final result was:

Sir John Dewar, Liberal   3918
Sir Reginald Macleod, Unionist   2774

The population of Inverness-shire at the 1911 census was 87,272, so a poll of only 6692 seems small after all the efforts made, even though women did not have votes. Probably the time of year and the scattered nature of the constituency would account for this.

1910: Our Fosterling, And First School Days

E arly in 1910 we had an interesting visitor: our Uncle Allan who was going to the United States to work for some years with Ford Motors braved the long winter journey from Paisley to Skye to see us before he left. He brought a romantic air of invention and travel into our quiet lives.

'We are all looking forward to Uncle Allan's visit. The children think he is a wonderful man, an engineer and maker of real motor cars. I was giving them a discourse on his moral and mental virtues the other day. Allan listened with all his eyes, and when I had done, asked in a solemn voice, "And has he got brown boots?" You never know what is passing through their heads!

'He will have a busy time when he comes, for all the inconvenient questions are being referred to him. As a specimen I may give one of Alasdair's. Yesterday he came down to the kitchen after me in a fearful hurry to ask, "Mama, what is free grace?" Isobel's troubles are of a different kind, but perhaps he can help her too. This was bothering her the other day. "Mama, I was reading in a magazine, 'Don'ts for Married Women', and it said, 'Don't speak to a man till he has eaten', but what are you to do if he isn't hungry?" What indeed?'

Perhaps I was rather young at six years old to be concerned with the problems of married women, but by that time I was reading anything I could lay my hands on. Mother describes my delight when she read me *Sir Patrick Spens*, and how next day she heard me repeating the first four stanzas to Alasdair. But writing and spelling were still a great trial to me — 'she has no patience if she can't do a thing at once' — and my growth in virtue and reverence left something to be desired.

'Alasdair is getting too pious to live. Today he said, "I like Sunday, not because I get my dinner downstairs, and not because I can play with the Bible picture-puzzle, but because it is God's day!" I saw future visions of a saintly youth in a pulpit, whereas a few days ago I had been willing to hand him over to Allan to make an engineer of him. If only Isobel had a little more of his spirit! When I was talking to her today of some of the Old Testament heroes she interrupted me to remark in a very cross voice:- "These old prophets! There's no end to them!" So if I am uplifted by the godliness of one child, I am kept humble by the impiety of another.'

The 26th of January was polling-day for the election in Skye, though results had come out more than a week before for less remote parts of the country. Mother's family in Paisley were fervent Liberals of the Scottish Nonconformist tradition, and she had been brought up in that political atmosphere, while father was so strongly Conservative that when a previous election went the other way he was so distressed as almost to make himself ill. The conflict of opinion might have become tense, but good humour prevailed: mother let them both have their heads but kept hers. Perhaps the fact that women did not have votes helped to preserve her calm. She writes on January 16th:-

'Our polling-day is not till the 26th, the last day possible, so the excitement will drag on till then. Ronald got the Saturday results this morning by telegram, and was rather disappointed with them. He feels very keenly about the issues at stake, as I have no doubt you do too in a different way. You both think that the hands of the clock will be put back if the other party gets in: indeed you are both sure of it. Perhaps in either case no such *tremendous* evils will happen as each of you expects. I can't help thinking that neither all the knaves nor all the heroes are to be found on one side, and that neither policy will bring in the millenium. You may blame me for sitting on the fence if you like, but perhaps it is the safest and most comfortable place when you have a husband on one side of it and a mother on the other'.

And two weeks later, on the 30th, she writes:- 'The excitement of this week was of course the Election. The children all marched out with blue ribbons in their button-holes as proud as Punch, and carried their Teddy Bears also decorated with blue ribbons. However their enthusiasm and their Daddy's hard work came to nothing, as you know. Ronald was not as downcast as he was last time, when he refused to take his food or speak to anyone. He was sorry, but took it more philosophically. He thinks it is no use now to contest the county so long as Sir John Dewar stands for it, as Sir Reginald was as strong a candidate as they could have. I am glad it is all over anyway'.

Towards the end of February mother and father went south and took Allan with them. 'I thought he would keep Ronald cheery during the long journey, and he is not much trouble', writes mother, picking up the three-year old child to put in their luggage as if it were a toy to amuse and distract her husband; but Allan was a gay handsome little boy who never ailed or wailed, and father was inclined to be morose towards the end of a long day of slow travel. They came home at the end of March, and there is a delightful picture of the enthusiastic welcome on the pier. One can see the cool spring sunshine on the rippling water, and the *Glencoe* paddling across the bay to the excited group.

'We got a beautiful day for the second part of the journey, but we had to take on over eight hundred sheep, so that we were very late in reaching our destination. The family was waiting for us on the pier, including wee Flora and Annie and Atten and Cousin Peter. The first thing we could see in the distance was Isobel dancing like a dervish, then before the boat could be moored greetings were shouted across to us, even Flora adding her voice to the chorus. "Wee Allan come home again! Wee Allan come home again!" Allan was the great toast, and got the warmest welcome. He in his turn shouted pieces of information from the boat, such as "I bought a watch in a shop!'' We made a triumphal procession home and got a further welcome from the girls there'.

But there had been sad news while they were away. Father's sister Mary who was married to Peter Martin of Cuidrach and had one child, Catriona or Trionag, had had a little boy, Peter, at Glenhinisdale, and soon after the birth had died of puerperal fever. Our parents decided to take this baby into their family, and mother discussed the matter with her maids to ensure their goodwill and friendly co-operation with her plan to bring another small child into a house where there were four already, the eldest being six years old. But she herself never had the slightest hesitation about adding a fifth child to her brood, even though Flora had only just passed her second birthday. There was plenty of room in her heart, and another cot could be fitted in somehow. It was also generous of Annie to stay with us in spite of the extra work, and the lure of £28 a year with her cousin in Glasgow. In the end she married a mason and went to live in Inverness.

'The girls had not heard about the baby. They took the news very nicely and said they would do their best for the wee boy. Annie, however, told me that her cousin wanted her to come south at the term — those provoking cousins! She is in a good house in Glasgow, getting £28 as a tablemaid, and wants Annie to come as head housemaid. I can see it is a tempting bait. She gets £18 from us, and I have offered to raise it to £19 (and I would almost be inclined to make it £20 if she would stay, but it seems a lot to give to one girl when one has three). She is considering the matter. I think she would like to oblige me, but of course I wouldn't want to stand in her way'.

So mother went to Glenhinisdale to bring home her fosterling. The poor little thing had been neglected in the alarm and sorrow of his mother's illness and death, so he was rather puny and fretful at first. I remember him arriving, a scrap of a thing, wrapped in a matted woollen shawl and accompanied by a heavy old-fashioned feeding-bottle with tubes inside it, which looked enough to give any infant the colic.

'The baby is a dear, with dark hair and bright eyes, a good nose and dimples. I took to him at once, and am as fond of him as I can be already. But he is very thin; I weighed him tonight, and he only weighs seven and a quarter pounds though he was four weeks old yesterday, so he looks rather like a skinned rabbit in his bath, but he seems quite strong. His lungs are all right anyway, and he makes good use of them. When we got home I gave him his bath and put him to bed and thought I had seen the last of him, but not a bit of it! He roared the whole evening, and kept Annie and me dancing attendance till ten o'clock I did not know how we were going to manage till someone suggested I should get a comforter. As you know, I have never used one, and was loth to break my rule, but I thought it would do him less harm than crying. It acts on him like a charm! After trying every possible method to quiet him and carrying him about in every position without any result, you have only to stick it in his mouth and he will lie down as quiet as a lamb.

'The children, especially Flora, are greatly taken up with him, but they have no idea of moderating their voices or making less noise on his account. I dare not take my eyes off Flora. She would like to hug him as she does our long-suffering cat'.

The new occupant of the pram caused much speculation in the village. Annie was evidently one who kept her mouth shut: if the inquisitive woman wanted to think that Mrs Macdonald had suddenly produced another child without any previous warning, let her! It was none of her business.

'He has been out every day since he came. The first day he went through the village he made a great sensation. Those who knew who he was looked on him with tender interest; those who did not were greatly astonished. Annie was amused at the inquiring looks she got. One woman ran up to her saying "Oh, I never heard that Mrs Macdonald had had a baby!" "Did you not?" said Annie. "It is a wonder I never heard!" "Yes, it is a wonder", said Annie, and passed on, leaving her staring.

'You will be glad to hear that Annie is staying. I said nothing more to her till tonight. I thought I would wait and see if the baby would appeal to her, and I am glad to say it does. It is very good of her to stay, as I know it is for my sake and the baby's and she will not have an easy time. It has been a great relief to my mind. Bella too has been very nice about it'.

Later in April she gives some of our reactions to the new arrival. 'Isobel was weeping because she wished the baby had been a girl. "He will grow up to be a boy, and then he will tease me, boo-hoo, boo-hoo!" She does sup sorrow with a long spoon! Allan too was annoyed at him the other day and flew into a passion. "He *shouldn't* have been born! Send him back to God! Send him back to God!" All the same they are very fond of him. Alasdair asked one day, "Mama, have all wee babies to be born?" and when I said yes he looked very thoughtful for a while and then said slowly, "Mama, I don't know what it is to be born"'.

Towards the end of April I went to school for the first time, and loved it. It was the old school under Fingal's Seat, a small massive building of grey granite quoined with red sandstone, now ruthlessly demolished to make way for a blank-faced structure of glass and concrete. The old stone building grew from the wild landscape of moors and heights that rose behind it: its impressive but useless tower and its gothic-arched sash windows suggested the dignity of learning. The A.B.C. class and the first two Standards were all taught in one long room with rising tiers of wooden desks and an iron stove, where dear Miss Robertson was infant-mistress, helped by boys and girls in their teens who were training as pupil-teachers. We found these rather dull, except dark-eyed gay Muriel Gillanders, the headmaster's daughter, whom we adored; it must have been a hard day's work for Miss Robertson to train them as well as teaching us. Her face was strong and tender, in ivory contrast to dark hair going grey; she had dark blue eyes with a hint of green in them and a humorous twinkle. She could comfort and encourage in Gaelic the little souls who came to her knowing no other language, but they had to pick up English before they moved on to the next room where Standards Three and Four were ruled by Miss Mackie who came from Aberdeen, knew no Gaelic and stood no nonsense.

There were no little chairs and tables; no pictures on the walls; no fun with water or clay or poster-paint. Our education was confined to the three Rs and religious knowledge. We began the day by saying the Lord's Prayer together. I had not met it before, and was full of awed delight in its words and its rhythm. Then we settled down to sums on slates, or to copy-books where pot-hooks and simple forms like *a* and *o* led our clumsy little fists to looped cursive script lines which proclaimed — 'Aberdeen, the Granite City', or 'Inverness, the Highland Capital'. I made short work of our reading-primers with their big print and bright pictures of apples or pussies or children at play, but sums and writing were more discouraging. One day Mr. Gillanders came to see how the infants were getting on; this was an honour, as he usually taught Latin and English to the senior classes. He squeezed his big form into one of the long desks, put an arm round me and asked what I was trying to write. When I murmured 'Capital Ds' he chuckled at my staggering and illegible efforts. 'Well, you *are* a funny little cup of tea', he said, and made a whole line of admirable letters, swinging round loops and curves with the greatest of ease. Sometimes on the long wet afternoons Miss Robertson played the piano and we did drill or had singing-games which made the time pass so quickly that we were surprised when the bell rang for going home.

Scripture lessons were easy because I knew all the stories already, but in the early Standards I met the Shorter Catechism and was not much impressed. No explanations were given; we simply memorised the answers by repeating them again in chorus. It would not have been easy to convey the abstract ideas of Calvinism to our infant minds, but the method led to some confusion. For instance, the first question is, 'What is man's chief end?' I thought I was being asked to define a magnificent new word — *manschyfen* — and swung with the others into a rhythmic chant — 'Manschyfen is to glorify God and to enjoy him for ever'. A few notes in our paper-covered penny Catechisms tried to give some help. '"End" means "Purpose". The end of a window is to let in light'. But as I misread the operative words as 'a widow' not much light was let in to my confused little mind.

Mother writes at the end of my first week. 'The family event has been the going to school of Isobel. She goes at 9.30 and gets back at 12.30, then she goes back at 2 o'clock till 3.30, so she has fairly long hours for a beginner. So far she has been greatly delighted with her experience. When she came home on the first day she ran upstairs crying, "Oh Mama, it is just *beautiful* at school!" Later I heard her tell someone that it was "gloriously fine", and again that "the school-mistress is every bit as nice as my own Mama!" The favourable impression has been kept up all week, and she has so much to tell when she comes home that I can hardly get her to eat her dinner. Miss

Robertson told Catriona that her arrival made quite a sensation at school. She heard one little boy say, "I know her", and another answer, "But I knew her before you, and I'll get taking her hand". She came home one day with a little paper boat one had presented to her, and told how another boy wanted to give her a paper basket, "but I didn't want it, and do you know what he did? He just tore it up!" So you see life begins early'.

But I did not enjoy school for long that spring; when I went out from my sheltered home atmosphere to this new world I met germs as well as education and romance, and was laid low with a severe type of influenza that ran through the house until by the end of May everyone had been ill except father, the baby Peter, now thriving in a climate of love and care, and Allan who was always healthy and cheerful. There were various complications; poor Flora developed an ear abscess, and as she was too little to tell what was wrong she could only express her misery by saying again and again in plaintive tones, 'I don't like it at all!' Medicine was lavishly prescribed in these days, and mother describes with some exasperation her difficulties in administering the doses.

'I do wish they would all get back to their normal again! I am sick and tired of going about with thermometers and medicine bottles. It is no joke, I assure you, to remember them all. Isobel has one bottle twice a day before food, one every three hours, one three times a day. Alasdair has one three times a day after food and one every few hours. Flora has one three times a day after food, and has her ear attended to twice a day, and Peter of course has a bottle every two hours, so I have to keep my wits about me. If they were all like Peter and supplied with an internal dinner-bell which refused to stop until attended to, it would not be so difficult'.

Towards the end of May an open-air memorial service for King Edward VII who had died three weeks earlier was held in the grassy arena with low rock walls leading to heathy slopes, and a view across the bay to the Cuillins. We all attended it, even Alasdair who was still in poor health, and the baby Peter in Annie's arms; it was an historic occasion, and mother thought he might like to tell his descendants that he had been there.

'We had a beautiful service on Friday; I don't think there could be many in the country more picturesque. It was held up the Lump on the games ground with the hills around us and the blue sky above. The Territorials had come in from all the country round, so we had over eighty with their bright scarlet and tartan making a brilliant line of colour on one side, then the Lovat Scouts with their faces as brown as their uniforms on the other, and between them the Free Masons with their blue sashes and aprons. All the school children were present, and nearly the whole of the community in spite of the fact that the Seceder minister would not join. There was a good choir, and the hymns and psalms with their minor tunes sounded very impressive'.

Annie went home to Staffin for her holidays and took Allan with her. 'Allan is looking the picture of health, sunburned and bonnie with his rosy cheeks and blue eyes. He is looking forward greatly to his visit to Staffin with his own "wee Annie". I would just as soon she had taken Alasdair, as Allan has been away already, but Allan is her own boy, and I could not suggest it'. Annie's widowed mother and a sister lived in a tiny thatched two-roomed cottage; its ruins can still be seen crouched under a spur of rock near the road at Culnaknock. There he slept in a built-in bed and played by the shore and had other interesting experiences. 'Allan came home from Staffin bursting with fat, which materially interfered with his good looks. I asked him how he had got so fat. "It was the eggs", he replied, and I discovered that he had eaten two a day all the time, and they had killed *three* hens for him. He enjoyed his visit very much. He was at church on Sunday for the first time. It was held in the schoolhouse, and he celebrated the event by upsetting an inkpot. "But", he explained, "the minister didn't see me". He and Flora had great chuckling and huggings over their reunion".

He still took an interest in his own appearance. 'Allan has been in great form lately, but he grows vainer every day. He weeps if he is not to be dressed for the afternoon, and he takes the greatest interest in every detail of his toilet, insisting on having everything to match, or "to fit", as he puts it. "I want these socks, for they fit this suit". His collar and tie are matters of great importance, and the other day when he was dressed in a clean suit and everything nice, he begged us to put gloves on him! Things reached a climax when Annie one day gave him a red and white striped sweet, and he begged us to put on his red and white striped suit "to fit it!" If the boy is father to the man, the only future I see for him is to tour the country as the best-dressed Highlander at his own expense. I found him trying to polish his nails with Daddy's manicure set. He is very gratified if you brush his hair with a silver-backed brush, and he can't bear sticky fingers. I'm afraid he is going to be a regular dandy!'

In August the Skye Games were held in the open-air arena, and mother remarks on the number of motor-cars to be seen in the street. 'I counted eight at one time from the library window'. Many more than eight could be counted on an August afternoon nowadays. Apparently there were comic turns as well as athletic events, and Allan was mystified by a clown. Daddy was becoming rather bald.

'I took the children in the forenoon and let the maids go out in the afternoon. The children enjoyed it, especially a very poor clown who could take his hair off, a thing which was very mysterious, and which they never doubted was genuine. Allan asked Daddy if he had taken his off. He did everything in dumb-show, so he wondered if he could speak, if he could eat, if he slept. He seemed to think it was a being from another world'.

During the summer Alasdair and I were taken south and spent several weeks with Grannie and the aunts in the Berwickshire fishing village of St. Abbs where they had rented a house. Here Aunt Jeanie took our education briskly in hand every morning: I was drilled in spelling and the multiplication table, and we both learned to write in slow and staggering fashion.

Mother had had a theory that the statutory age of five was too early for a child to begin school, and in these days compulsion could be avoided if some lessons were given at home. I was six and a half when I made my first appearance at school, and was immediately attacked by the severe and lingering influenza which infected the whole family. I was not well enough to go back during the summer term, which in Scotland ends in June, so I did not begin regular education till I was seven years old, in September 1910. Alasdair, aged five, started at the same time, as mother's theory about late beginnings and the danger of fatigue vanished before the practical convenience of getting rid of a child or two for much of the day, and the discovery that far from being exhausted we were immensely stimulated and as happy as larks. Although I could read with great fluency, my late start made it a hard struggle to match children of my own age in arithmetic, writing and spelling and it was humiliating to find clever little Alasdair, who was two years younger, treading on my heels and breathing down my neck all through our primary years — indeed, in 1914 when I was ten and he was eight we were in the same classroom for a time. Mother describes his first weeks. I am afraid his shocking remark about the crab was deliberate, for he has always had a quietly comic streak, turning up an innocent face and making everyone laugh.

'The two older children are still enjoying school, though there was a slight protest from Alasdair on Friday morning — "But I don't want to go to school every day!" From what I hear he seems to be a bit of a pickle. Isobel came home rather indignant one day and told us Alasdair had made them all laugh in the Bible Lesson. "It was about the baptism of Jesus, and the teacher asked what had happened when Jesus stepped into the river. And instead of saying that God's soul descended on him like a dove Alasdair said that a crab bit his toes!" I don't think the wee boy knew the story in spite of his mother's upbringing, and I expect that after five weeks at St Abbs he thought it was a much more likely thing to happen'.

On a Saturday in mid-September we had a happy excursion to the west side of the island, to Dunvegan and home by Bracadale and Sligachan. The road climbs towards Glen Drynoch above the long grey arm of Loch Harport, with the rocky sgurrs of the Black Cuillins standing dramatically against the sky. Here an accident occurred that might have been serious if Allan's head had struck a rock instead of the grassy bank at the side of the road.

'Yesterday Ronald had business on the other side of the island, so we took a motor and the three older children and went round by Dunvegan and home by Sligachan. We had our picnic-dinner on the hillside, and when we came to the beautiful bridge of Drynoch we climbed down to the water's edge and up to the waterfall. Then we had rather an unpleasant adventure. The children were very eager to sit in front, and as the chauffeur assured us it was quite safe we allowed them to do it. When we started from Drynoch Alasdair and Allan were in front. The driver swerved to avoid something on the road, and you can imagine our feelings when we suddenly saw Allan disappear over the side of the car! In a moment there was a yell from the rear — most welcome sound! — the driver had the car into the ditch in his excitement, and Ronald and I had jumped over the side without waiting to open the door, and had picked up the poor wee chap. Fortunately he had fallen on the step first and just rolled off, otherwise I shudder to think what the consequence might have been. As it was he escaped with a bump on his head and a bit of a shock. After the first yell he was dazed and a little sick. I wanted to get him home quickly and put him to bed, but he slept on my knee all the way from Sligachan, and wakened when we got to Portree as brisk as a lark, ready for a good tea and quite himself. Today he and Alasdair were having a discussion about what they were going to do "next time I fall out of a motor" or "when I fall out of a motor". There will be no next time if I can prevent it'.

Alasdair and I continued to speculate and to ask difficult questions. 'Isobel remarked to me today, "There is one thing that puzzles me very much. Who made God?" Alasdair too has his problems, but it is the Divine Omnipotence that exercises him. "Can Jesus see his own nose?" he asked me quite seriously.'

She then mentions Lord Pentland's visit and the long talk he had with father before going down to discuss the crofters' grievances at Idrigill. Father had his own troubles, since new methods of land-taxation had come in and he and Mr. Fraser had to supply details of the holdings on all the estates for which their firm acted.

'Ronald's attitude towards your friend Lloyd George is, to say the least, not very Christian. They have just got something like 3,000 forms from the office, which are so complicated that they must be filled up either by himself or Mr. Fraser. Each takes over an hour to do, and means a lot of looking up books and worry. They must all be done within thirty days with a penalty of up to £50 for the neglect of any one. Of course it is physically impossible even working night and day to do this, and they have written to explain as much. The form must be filled in for every little tumbledown croft. You can understand the irksomeness of the task, especially as Ronald is convinced that whatever may be said for the scheme as applied to towns it is utterly unnecessary and useless here — and the irksomeness is not lessened by the fact that he does not get a penny extra for doing it, and that it comes at a particularly busy time with other work. So I think he may be forgiven if his language when speaking of the Chancellor of the Exchequer is somewhat forceful at times'.

Alasdair was a friendly little soul, but he seemed to prefer rough boys to smooth ones, which made it awkward for mother who did not want to seem snobbish, but was reluctant to have her garden overrun with young toughs. There really was a poor insane man called daft Norman, who lurked in the wood peering and muttering, and inspired our extraordinary tales of prowess and danger. His face was dead white with a black beard, so my description was accurate enough, though it must have sounded like pure fantasy.

'The children are still enjoying school, though the other morning Alasdair had a terrible sore throat and a fearful sore ear about 9.30 which passed away as the day wore on. He is a great boy for inviting all the little ragamuffins in the school to come and play in our garden, At the dinner-hour there will be three or four of the noisiest and raggedest boys in the school making no end of a row. I have to make a rule that no boy is asked in without permission, but they stand outside waiting to be asked. It is not easy to know what to do in a place like this.

'Another trouble is the stories they come home with. They came in the other day with eyes wide with excitement, saying there was a "daft man" in the wood. Isobel declared that she had seen him and he had nothing on but his shirt. Next day her story was that he had run after Nanette Macrae and flung his long knife at her, and if she had been nearer she would have been killed. Later he had been seen jumping over the bridge into a lot of nettles — "and that story is true because we saw where the nettles were crushed down!" — and Alasdair Lamont, a brave youth in the class above Alasdair's, had seen him running across the river, and he fired twice at him with his gun, and then he ran away with yells and cries and disappeared into the wood, but Alasdair Lamont threw a stone at him and hit him on the leg. His appearance according to Isobel was "too horrible to be described — his face was half black and half white". Did you ever hear such blethers? I forbade them to mention the daft man, but before you can stop them out comes something more about him. For the last day or two, however, I have heard nothing, so I trust he is forgotten'.

In late October the three maids all informed mother that they were leaving at 'the term', which must have been the Martinmas term next month. 'The solid earth seemed to be sinking under my feet'. Annie did not want to leave, but her sister was tired of being at home and wanted Annie to change with her: mother promised a rise and persuaded her to stay. Bella who had been with us for five and a half years felt she had learned all she could and wanted more experience, so we parted with regrets and good wishes. The cook, Mary Ann, had not settled in very well, so was not so much of a loss, but 'her place is not easy to fill', and indeed the letter goes on to describe the fiasco of an elaborate dinner, probably of five or six courses, which had been prepared for a Major Gunn who had come to lecture to the Territorials and was staying in the Royal Hotel.

'I had no end of trouble and worrying getting things nice. I was in despair about fish till I managed to secure some flounders. Then I made the puddings myself, and hunted about for fruit, and spent the whole day arranging flowers and looking after things. I had everything completed to my satisfaction and was just going to rush away to dress when Ronald came in and told me *he was not coming!* Like the man in the story 'he wasn't hungry'. He was anxious about his lecture and his limelight views, and preferred just having some tea in the hotel. You can imagine how flat I felt. And the worst of it was that he said he would come in afterwards, so we had not only to eat our grand dinner by ourselves, but I had to arrange a supper for him later. However he was very nice indeed when he did come, and we enjoyed meeting him'.

By the middle of November mother had engaged two new maids — both from Raasay! Mary Gillies the new housemaid was not altogether a success, but the cook Julia Nicolson, was a dear. Mary Ann's attitude to children had been, 'Out of my kitchen, the lot of you!' so when we heard that there was a new cook we stole down the back stairs from the nursery landing to peep at her through the bannisters. When she saw the little faces peering she cried out with a strong Highland accent, 'Children! It is the children! Come down now — come you here to me!' and opened her arms to hug us. She was always welcoming, good-natured and ready for a laugh; she put us up to tease Annie by asking innocent questions about her mason. She also turned out to be a very good cook with a real interest in her work and in learning new recipes. Mother describes their first interview.

'I have engaged the Raasay girl, Julia Nicolson. She came over to see me on Monday night, walking nine miles in drenching rain and crossing in a wild storm, so I think she deserved the place. In any case she seemed suitable. She has had a good deal of experience as housekeeper-general and laundry-maid, and when she told me she *loved* washing I could not engage her quickly enough lest wings should develop and she should fly away. She was not at all greedy about wages either, evidently wanting to prove her worth before asking too much. Altogether I feel hopeful about her, and as she is very friendly with Mary the other new girl, and both are friends of Annie, I hope we shall have a peaceful winter'.

And next week she describes how they are settling in. 'I have had a busy week getting my new maids into shape. During the first day or two it was, "Change and decay in all around I see", and I felt as if I would never get things right, but now I feel more hopeful. Julia is a big slow girl who gives you the impression at first that she is stupid, but I think she will be all right once she gets to know the work, and she seems reliable. Mary, I think, will make a good housemaid; she is smart with her work, and of course they are both anxious to please at present. They suffer from the disadvantage of being more used to Gaelic than English, which makes it difficult for them to follow a quickly given order. Annie has been a tower of strength to me these days; I don't know what I would have done if she had left too. She can explain things to them so much better than I can'.

Meanwhile we soldier on at school. 'The children had some wild weather this week to go through. One morning Alasdair wanted to stay at home, but his imagination was not active enough to supply an excuse. "I'm awfully sore", he whimpered, "but I don't know where it is. I think I've forgotten". Then pointing to his ribs, "Yes, it's there". But the first thing he said when he came home was, "It was *beautiful* at school today!"

66

'Isobel went through a hedge and tore her new waterproof from top to bottom in two places. She was very tearful about it, and offered to empty her money-box to pay to have it mended. She also broke a hand-basin, so she has been unlucky this week. "Oh, if I could have died before this happened!" she wailed. "If my tears could only mend it! Why did I not die when I was a baby!" I wonder what she will do when the real troubles come.'

It is difficult for grown-ups to realise what a shock a piece of accidental damage can be to a child. You, you alone have broken this useful and familiar object; you did not mean to, but it can never be mended. It is like killing something. There is usually a scolding to be taken as well, but that is not the only reason for the feeling of profound grief and horror which I expressed so vividly. A week later I was being very perverse.

'Isobel is in one of her cantankerous moods today. Instead of having a "service" she wanted to institute a worship of the Golden Calf. "Oh Golden Calf, thou didst make us! We praise thee!" — and so on. Then she got her hymn-book and tried to alter the hymns into praise of the Golden Calf, and was not at all pleased when I put a stop to it. You know how she tries to wriggle out of all responsibility for her own naughtiness — "You shouldn't have allowed me to do it!" — or words to that effect. The other night she had been naughty and I went down after she was in bed to have a little motherly talk with her. I found her still unrepentant, and she went back to first causes. "Well, Adam and Eve shouldn't have eaten that apple and then I wouldn't have done it. I wish they hadn't been the first man and the first woman . I asked her if she thought she would have done any better if she had been there. "Yes. I would have cut down the tree". I pointed out that they had no axes in these primitive times, but she had her answer ready. "Well, I would have got a beaver to bite through it"'

This year Grannie and the aunts clubbed together to give us a magnificent Christmas present — a rocking-horse covered in sleek brown pony-skin and mounted on a stand so that we could not rock ourselves over. Mother wrote to thank her family: 'I wish you had been there when it was presented to see the delight it gave. I was afraid there might be ructions among my little spitfires in their eagerness to enjoy it, but there was nothing of the kind. Alasdair gallantly remarked, "I think Flora should get the first ride". "I quite agree with you, Alasdair", said Isobel. However it was an honour that Flora did not covet. Nothing on earth would induce her to risk her life on its back, so Allan was next voted to be first. His enjoyment is a little mixed with fear so far. The other two like to pretend it is bolting with them, but Allan says, "I like it to bolt slowly"'.

Dr. Dewar who had died in 1909 had been succeeded by Dr. Fletcher who was skilled and reliable, but in October of this year he had been appointed Medical Officer of Health for Skye, and to everyone's dismay the new general practitioner in Portree was a young man just out of college. 'We are all hoping we keep well for the next few years', says mother. Just before Christmas she had to call him in.

'On Monday, Mary, my new housemaid, took ill; her face and especially her nose was very swollen, and she had to go to bed. By the evening her temperature was 102, and she felt so miserable that I sent for the doctor. I was afraid of erysipelas. He did not come till next day, but he said it was not that, but a swelling of mucous membrane of the nose following influenza, and he would come twice a day to paint and syringe it. We have a new doctor now; he is twenty-three and only finished last spring, so he is still pretty spring-like. There ought to be a law that doctors should either take a first place as an assistant, or start in a town where you can take them or leave them. It seems absurd to give a mere boy the full charge of a big district where you have no choice. He took Mary's case very seriously and suggested horrifying possibilities. First, he said, there was such a thing as nasal diphtheria. "Of course it is very rare, but we must watch for that" — but I could hardly keep my face straight when after the girl was getting on splendidly with almost normal temperature he cheerily remarked that there were three possible developments — meningitis, pneumonia and Bright's disease! He might just as well have finished up with phthisis and cancer: they looked quite as likely. He gave her five bottles of stuff and then suggested she might have a stimulant. I asked in a surprised voice if he thought it was necessary. "Of course the medical profession is dead against it", he said. I thought it was absurd to order one for a strong healthy girl who had only been a day or two in bed and to whom he was already giving a tonic of iron, quinine and strychnine. She was up on Thursday and is feeling quite ready for her work, though her nose is still swollen. I feel more than ever I don't want to be ill for a while'.

The new doctor was not only an alarmist but extremely careless to leave a bottle of poison behind in a house full of children. Mother used to recall how Annie came into the library that winter afternoon dead-white and almost speechless with horror, holding out the empty bottles. Allan, now four years old, was a lively adventurous little boy; he probably felt guilty at pouring out the medicine and became confused by Annie's alarmed questioning.

'And now I must tell you of a terrible fright we got yesterday. The doctor brought two small bottles with him to paint Mary's nose, and kept them on the mantelpiece of the pink room where I was nursing her. Yesterday Annie came to me with the two bottles empty, and said she had asked Allan about them, and he said that Flora and he had drunk them. As one of them was marked "Poison" you can imagine my feelings. When I questioned Allan he said he hadn't drunk it all, but put some of it on the floor. Ronald went at once to the chemist who told him that Allan couldn't have drunk any of it, for it was a deadly poison and its action was immediate. But it had practically no taste, and there was nothing but a watchful Providence to prevent Flora and him from drinking the bottle between them. I couldn't sleep for thinking what a terrible Christmas we might have had. He is such a pickle; only that morning he had tried to put paraffin on the nursery fire but luckily the can was empty. He doesn't mean to be naughty, but you never know what he will do next'.

1911: Coronation, Church Union and Comets

Early in the new year Flora and Peter had wheezing colds and high temperatures. Rather reluctantly mother called in her medical adviser again; he told her that Flora had pleurisy and the baby bronchitis. 'Fortunately my former experience had accustomed me to his way of calling a spade an agricultural implement, so I was not quite so alarmed as I might have been'. Sure enough when he came next day both children were much better. 'Did you ever hear of pleurisy making a weekend visit like that?' asks mother. 'If I had not got the doctor, in my ignorance I would have called it a feverish cold'.

From an early age Alasdair had a great interest in sewing which mother encouraged as it kept him busy and happy. When father teased him about this unmasculine pursuit he had an answer ready.

'Alasdair is very fond of sewing, and has been pestering me to get him another mat to do. Daddy was teasing him and asking him why he liked to sew. His reply was, "I want to learn to sew so that when I get married and my wife dies I won't have to marry another'. There is no harm in looking well forward!'

At the end of January a military funeral was held in the overgrown graveyard on the other side of our garden wall. As a captain in the territorial battalion of the Queen's Own Cameron Highlanders father wore his scarlet and tartan uniform; there were pipes and drums, and we had an excellent view of it all from the nursery window. My shocking idea of a hell peopled entirely by children did not cause us the least concern; we were sheltered by the affection that surrounded us from any morbid fears of hell or the devil. Our speculations were interesting but never painful: God and Jesus would protect us from all harm, just as our parents would.

'The children were all excited this week over a military funeral that was given to a poor man who had been a soldier in his youth. They helped Daddy to dress, and then they began to speculate. "Does a man's soul go to Jesus when he dies?" asked Alasdair. I said it did. Then he wanted to know if the soldier had been a good man. I hesitated, for as a matter of fact he had been no better than he should be. Isobel saved the situation by remarking emphatically, "Alasdair, of course all *big* people go to heaven when they die; it's only children who are naughty". Allan finished by remarking cheerfully, "Mama, I know two dead people; Atten's auntie and Alasdair Whiteford's father"'

School was still a great interest, but any shinty played by Alasdair at the age of five must have been hopeful knockabout with a ball, some other little boys and a curved stick. We did not have a regular gymnastic mistress in Portree till 1913 when the quadrangle in the middle of our school was roofed over to make a gymnasium, and the new science block was built at the side; the young lady must have been a visiting teacher. Father found it strange that games should be taught in school-time when they had been sternly discouraged in his much harder youth.

'Allan is already longing to go to school. One day I found him with his coat on higgelty-piggelty going off in his slippers after Alasdair. If you saw Alasdair setting out merrily with his shinty-club in his hand you would know what his opinion was on the subject. We have had a young lady here for the last few weeks teaching Swedish drill and games to the children. They do get well looked after! Ronald remarked that these were changed days; they now give a big salary to a lady to teach children to play, whereas in his early days if they were caught playing they were whipped'.

But I was sorrowful when Evie Calder and Nanette Macrae got tired of sharing the fantasy-life that was so real to me. I could have set witch-traps or built fairy-houses for weeks on end.

'Isobel came home from school in a very depressed and rather tearful mood. Her two little chums, Evie and Nanette, had run away from her. "We were playing at witch-traps, and I was busy making one, and when I looked round they weren't there, and Alasdair said he saw them running round the corner, and (more tearfully) I thought they were interested in the witch-traps". For several days I had heard a lot about these witch-traps. They had gathered together some old tins and broken ends of bottles which they filled with water and sank here and there in a meadow; then they carefully covered them with moss, put a withered leaf in the centre of each with a little piece of yellow whin on the top of the leaf. The whin, which was fairy gold, was supposed to attract the greedy witches as they stepped across the meadow at night, and as soon as they stood on the withered leaf they fell into the water underneath and were caught in the trap. I don't know what the others believed, but Isobel declared they caught the witches and drowned them in a muddy pool. After two or three days the others must have got tired of the game, but Isobel was very much hurt. "It's so disappointing", she said pathetically'.

In March the Communion time came round again, and mother had a little grumble about her minister. 'I don't know where Mr. Macleod picks up the ministers he gets to assist, but as a rule they are very dry sticks. We are not always pleased with him either. Today I knew every word of his sermon, I had heard it so often. I believe one faithful hearer who marks his Bible has fifteen dates opposite one text. Today he had changed his text, but it was exactly the same sermon, and as the last time I heard it was just before the New Year it was rather soon to have it again'.

Grannie came up from the Glen and her services were as long as ever. 'She has been nearly four hours away already, and there is no word of her coming home, or of our dinner for which we are now beginning to feel very ready. She went off before eleven, and it is now four. If we are hungry what must she be? — for we had some lunch between times'. One cannot help wondering what the Seceder ministers found to say during these protracted services, just as one wonders how Palmertson managed to speak for five hours on the Don Pacifico incident. Some of the time would be spent in droning through long stretches of the metrical psalms, but all prayers and sermons had to be extempore. Probably a good deal of vain repetition took place to pad out the devotions, in spite of their dislike of a formal liturgy.

Mother found her own Communion service more satisfying than she expected, but on coming home she had a shock. Allan had been experimenting again; he was such a lively eager little boy that we never knew what he would do next. Willie the gardener called him 'the wicked fellow'. Flora had soft straight light-brown hair that was inclined to straggle into points and look untidy.

'I came home from church feeling at peace with all the world, but my peace was rudely broken when I entered the house by a vision of Flora looking like a moulting canary, and informing me that Allan had cut off her hair in the bathroom. The culprit had already been dealt with by his father, so I was spared that pain, but oh, I feel vexed! Her hair has always been troublesome and was just beginning to get more manageable, and now I don't know what to do with it. If I were near a hairdresser I would have it all cut short, but it is not easy to do that myself, and meantime she is a beauty!'

However it was for the best in the end. 'I cut Flora's hair quite short, and we all agree that it is the greatest improvement. She looks much smarter and tidier and bonnier. Ronald felt he should apologise to Allan for the whipping, and treat him as a public benefactor'. Nowadays there would have been no problem, but at that time even tiny girls had to have long hair.

We were surrounded by interesting books and never saw a comic or a cartoon-strip. Mother read us *The Pilgrim's Progress* on Sundays about this time, and in the evenings there were the *Jungle Books* and the Ernest Thomson Seton stories — *Lives of the Hunted* and *Monarch the Big Bear*. There is an amusing glimpse of father instructing us in history.

'Ronald is reading to the children about the Charge of the Light Brigade. Alasdair came home from school saying that Miss Robertson has told them about the "Battle of Light". From his description we recognised what he meant, and Daddy further explained it to him. Allan was greatly interested, and next day asked Daddy to tell him the "story of the Battle of Night and Day." You see what accurate minds my sons have! Daddy is explaining it with the aid of bricks, and they are all eagerly following it'.

As our sweets were strictly rationed to one or at most two a day and we had no pocket-money to buy any, we should all have had excellent teeth, but though Flora, Allan and I had very little trouble, Alasdair and Peter had to endure much suffering because of the dentist's infrequent visits. He arrived in March of this year. 'The event of this week was the visit of the dentist. He comes twice a year, so I thought I would have the children's teeth examined. Isobel's lower ones are coming in very irregularly. She has such good teeth that the old ones do not make way for the new, but she has not a speck of decay in any of them. Alasdair has two back teeth beginning to go. I was amused at the difference between the two children. Isobel had to have an eye-tooth taken out, and though it was deadened she was in a perfect panic over it. Alasdair on the other hand never turned a hair though he had the birling machine into him. He seemed quite interested'.

Early in April there is a letter of varied news. The road by Loch Fada which would eventually reach Staffin rose steadily to the wild moors below the precipices and pinnacles of Storr. Beyond the town reservoir it was only a half-made track; difficult going for young Allan even though refreshments were handed round before we turned homeward. It is interesting that a small boy's reefer coat was then considered an extravagant purchase at 19/6d.

'Yesterday the children had a long walk with their Daddy to the nearest Storr Loch along the road that is in process of construction. Ronald as Clerk to the County Council likes to go and inspect it periodically. He had Allan with him as well as Isobel and Alasdair, and over eight miles of rough walking was a good deal, I thought, for a child of four, especially as he has to keep trotting all the time to keep pace with his Daddy's long strides. They came back from the loch in an hour and twenty minutes, and he was pretty tired, but very well pleased with himself. I asked him what he liked best in the walk; his answer was, "The biscuits". So his heart is in the right place for a small boy, though he might have had them at home without so much trouble.

'I bought Alasdair's summer reefer coat this year instead of making it, and he is immensely proud of it, especially of the three pockets, which are the envy of the other members of the family whose home-made coats are sadly lacking in pockets. It cost 19/6d, so I am afraid the others will have to be content with pocketless coats a bit longer.

'Isobel lost her two front upper teeth this week, which gives her a rakish look and a lisp. Aunt Agnes will sympathise with her, and appreciate her remark at tea, "My food is just a burden to me for want of these teeth!" I wonder whether she or Aunt Agnes will get fixed up first. As baby added a tooth to his store this week the dental total of the family is not much reduced'.

Alasdair continued to knit. It was a useful accomplishment which he did not forget; during the last war he helped his wife to knit outfits for their little twin daughters. 'Alasdair has started a pair of cuffs for Glen Grannie and works at them by fits and starts, but as his favourite position while knitting is stretched on his back on floor or sofa with his heels in the air his progress is not very fast. He has begun to take an interest in books now that he can read a little, and spends a long time slowly spelling out line after line of *Swiss Family Robinson* or *The Water Babies*'. He was big-hearted as well as persevering. 'He was in one of his generous moods today, and was telling me what he would do when he grew up. "And I'll send a rocking-horse to the little children you'll have then, and if your husband is poor I'll send him iron to make engines of". So old age need have no terrors for me'.

In May spring-cleaning was in full swing again, and mother hired a primitive vacuum-cleaner that worked by pumping. We must have had our Easter holiday late that year, as we were all under foot until we discovered the balcony halfway down the red stairs. It usually held ferns and aspidistras, and the tall window of ground glass was edged with blue and red panes each portraying a lily.

'We had a vacuum-cleaner for a day and a half, called the Daisy. I got Willie to work it for part of the time and he did not like it at all — said he would rather beat six carpets than do one with the vacuum. It really was very hard work and terribly uninteresting but it had got out a good deal of dirt when we came to examine the bag. In one way it was a great advantage. It poured all week from Sunday to Sunday, so without it we could not have got on at all, as we could get nothing out. And if we could not get the carpets out we could not get the children out either. They were having a fine old time of it, in everybody's way and up to every mischief. Nobody had time to find employment for them except Satan.

'Fortunately they discovered a grand playground in the staircase window. The plants had been all taken away, leaving a broad shelf with a railing round it, and by means of a ladder formed by the side of the crib they climbed up and down. Sometimes it was a castle, sometimes a boat, when they would sit and fish with bits of string. They piled it up with the library cushions and made themselves very comfortable. Even Flora managed with Alasdair's help to climb into it, but she could not get out, so periodically there were plaintive whines — "I want to get down!" — and someone had to go to the rescue. It was rather a dangerous playground, but I was so thankful to get them out of the way that I took the risk'.

Mother went south in June, taking the three older children with her. The two little boys were left in Paisley, and I was dropped at Birmingham to stay with Uncle Robbie and Aunt Margaret while mother and Aunt Agnes went to London to stay with Uncle George and see the Coronation of King George V and Queen Mary. On that journey I had my first experience of a restaurant-car: to feast on roast mutton and gooseberry tart with cream while the train climbed Shap summit was the greatest luxury after egg sandwiches and cocoa from the thermos on the West Highland line. Then I met my cousin Alice for the first time; she was a long-haired charmer of six years old, and as we both loved telling stories and writing poems, we got on very well. I had so many exciting experiences in Birmingham that for a long time the three heavy syllables of its name sounded as exotic and storied as Baghdad or Pekin. I was taken to the Botanic Gardens where in a huge glass-house I saw a pink water-lily with leaves so big that a small child could sit on one, and we bought a postcard which showed that very thing. There was also a Zoo where I gazed with fear and wonder at a coiled-up boa-constrictor. Aunt Margaret took us to the swimming-baths one morning, but that was too much for me. Bathes in Skye had been few, and this great hall full of water slapping against the tiled sides, and echoing with the cries and splashes of the bathers filled me with panic. Little Alice jumped in fearlessly and practised her strokes in the shallow end; bold Arthur, her nine-year-old brother, swam a length, but I clung to Aunt Margaret in tears, and did not dare to go in except for one small dip with her arms round me. But Coronation Day itself was a more successful treat: we were taken into the town after dark for the festivities. There were crowds all round laughing and singing: soldiers marched and bands played, and lights whirled round portraits of our new King and Queen, and for the final wonder we were lifted up on shoulders to see the Illuminated Tram Car which rocked and twanged along the street outlined in many-coloured glory.

Having crossed the border to England and stayed in one of its major cities I was considered a much-travelled child when I came back to Skye. One day next summer when Evie and Nanette and I were playing near the bridge during our morning-break a group of sentimental tourists got into conversation with us. 'Islanders!' said one lady, sighing deeply. 'Children of Skye who have never left their island!' We resented this. 'I was born in Thurso', said Evie. 'And I've been to Glasgow', said Nanette. 'And I've stayed for two weeks in Birmingham', I said, swelling with pride. Collapse of romantic tourist.

I was picked up and brought back to Paisley, but the radiant Coronation summer of travel and sunshine was not yet over; we all went for some weeks to a house that Grannie had taken at Kildonan, Isle of Arran. It stood by a wide empty beach of sand where we paddled and splashed all day; there were rocky pools where fish darted and hermit-crabs lurched along in the clear water. I had a special pool where I watched the tides come and go; I amused Aunt Agnes by remarking one day that I thought the sea-anemones in it were getting to know me. At dusk the mysterious beam of light-houses on Pladda and Ailsa Craig flashed over the calm sea. Our eye-surgeon uncle George was there too; he played tunes on his flute, and he burned our names on the top of our wooden spades with a burning-glass, controlling it with delicate care as he controlled his instruments in critical operations on the eye. We felt he was a man in touch with cosmic powers as he held the glass steadily to the sun, and 'Isobel' and 'Alasdair' gradually appeared in strongly outlined brown letters with a tiny fume of smoke.

At the end of September after we had come home I had my eighth birthday, and mother wrote, 'I am glad you are sending Isobel a book, for it is pathetic to see how her small library is read and re-read. Her Daddy's library is rather beyond her yet, but once she finds her way there she will have food enough. I gave her one of Maria Edgeworth's books today, and she has almost finished it'. And two weeks later, 'Isobel is delighted with *Little Lord Fauntleroy*. Her criticism of it today was, "I think it is the most interesting book I ever read, after the *Iliad* and the *Odyssey*". So you see she places it pretty high'.

I was comparing it with the versions of Homer based on the Butcher and Lang translations which were published in the *Told to the Children* series, of which we had a number of books. I was a voracious reader, but I had more varied food than mother suggests, since father had bought the whole original series of *Everyman's Library* when it first came out at a shilling a volume, including all the section of children's books. We had the *Annals of Fairyland* in the reigns of King Oberon, King Cole and King Herla; *Granny's Wonderful Chair*, *The Girlhood of Shakespeare's Heroines*, and Jules Verne's enthralling series which begins with *Dropped from the Clouds*, to name only a few.

Allan continued to be interested in dress. 'He found an old dirty frayed-out collar in a corner of the garden, and the delight it has given him is beyond words. He washed it after his own fashion and put it out to dry. He wanted to have it on when he went for his walk, but I drew the line there. His idea was: "When I go out with the collar on, people will see it, and they will ask me how old I am, and when I say I am only four they will be surprised that I have a collar". He made me promise to give him a box of studs for his birthday, and remarked quite seriously, "When I grow up I won't have to buy so many collars, for I will have this one'. Altogether the amount of pleasure and jumping for joy it has given him would surprise anyone who did not know Allan's vanity and his passion for nice things of his own'. But he was a generous-hearted little boy too. 'He is ambitious to be another Carnegie. He gleefully remarked yesterday, "Mama, when I grow up I am going to give everyone in the world half-a-crown!" — then he danced on his toes in anticipation of the universal joy'.

During the shooting season mother was gratified though sometimes embarrassed by presents of game from father's friends and clients. Grouse, snipe, hares and salmon were very welcome, but venison was another matter. In October she writes. 'I assure you I did not impoverish myself in sending you the venison. A huge haunch of venison is apt to hang heavily on the mind of a housekeeper, but when one is presented with two haunches on the same day the problem assumes alarming proportions. You can picture me standing before the kitchen table, knife in hand, with half a stag before me, wondering what in the world I am to do with the beast. We had already disposed of a haunch, so that you might say we are responsible for three-quarters of a deer. I am not particularly fond of venison in any case, and am quite thankful when after various roasts and stews and pies and soups we see the end of it. I hope we have come to the end of our friends' generosity in that line, for I feel as if the ghost of the noble animal will haunt me if I have to face a fourth quarter'.

Mother decided to change her housemaid Mary at the November term; she had become moody and difficult, and mother was not satisfied with her way with the children. Unfortunately our dear Julia also had to go. 'She is as sorry about it as I am, but a younger sister insists on going out to service, and her father says she must come home. She doesn't want to leave a bit, and I'm sure I don't want to part from her. She is the best girl I ever had in the kitchen, and I had got her so nicely into my ways. She had quite a taste for cooking, and was pleasant in the house and with the children, and now I shall have to begin all over again with a girl who only knows how to make broth and pea soup'. Mary was replaced by Annie Sutherland who stayed with us for several years. She was a very reliable and pleasant girl; we called her Nana to distinguish her from the other Annie. We had a stop-gap cook for some time, and then next year Julia managed to come back to us, warmly welcomed by everyone.

But before they left, Hallowe'en was celebrated in the big stone-floored kitchen, with a blazing fire in the range and the lamps placed on high shelves so that their globes would not be cracked by splashes of water from the tub where we ducked or forked for apples. Peter was tucked up in bed, but everyone else took part, except father who was too sedate for such frolics. 'We had a great time last night with the children, keeping Hallowe'en. It is the first time we have held it, so everything was new, not only to the children but to the bigger children in the kitchen. I wish you could have seen us; such shouting, laughing, shrieking and dancing! Flora would hold the fork with the prong against the button she calls her nose instead of the handle, and Annie who has short lips and prominent teeth couldn't catch the nuts at all, and Julia always choked and came out with a fearful explosion, and Isobel got her whole head under the water after apples till her very ribbon was soaking, and everyone got several apples except poor Mama who only got one. And Flora and Allan stayed up till half-past-seven, and both ate more apples and nuts than were altogether good for them, and everyone was fearfully happy, and the children are wondering when we will play that game again'.

In mid-October I was advanced to Standard III, and moved into Miss Mackie's room. Children did not go up by years in the primary department of Portree school; they were moved when their teacher thought they were ready. I spent two years with Miss Mackie; Alasdair only six months. She was the most elderly and the least interesting of our teachers: pale and portly with grey hair done up in puffs, a high-necked blouse and a voluminous skirt with a broad leather belt where they joined. She kept good order and drilled us well, but her methods were repetitive and monotonous: when an Inspector walked in one morning and gave us a lively lesson about the countries round the Baltic Sea it was like rain in the desert. I came home full of conceited glee. 'The Inspector was telling us about the Laplanders, and he asked what animals they kept, and all the children said, "Polar bears", but I said "Reindeer", and he said I was a clever little girl, and oh! he was such a nice man!'

Teachers had to be versatile in those days. I remember the elderly Miss Mackie giving us lessons in Swedish drill. We were lined up on the classroom floor and she stood on the top step of the desk-tiers doing energetic arm-movements or stooping and straightening with a will while we followed her count. When she taught the girls sewing she had to keep a stern eye on the boys who were doing sums on the other side of the room, and ply the tawse at the first sign of disorder. Sometimes tattered books were handed round for 'silent reading', which would give her a breather. We had to take these books as we were given them and no arguing: there was one story about a little girl who stole a plum which all my friends said was wonderful, but it never came my way.

Meanwhile Alasdair and Miss Robertson were great friends. 'He brought her a great rusty pin the other day, and told her to keep it for it was a good thing for taking out stabs'. And in October: 'He was explaining to his teacher that the reason there was no king in Queen Elizabeth's time was that it was long ago before there were any husbands. The first day they had a fire he remarked to her, "Isobel's mother was asking if they had a fire in Miss Mackie's room". Haven't they a funny way of putting things?' And a month later. 'Miss Robertson was quoting a remark of Alasdair's today. He was telling her about our latest kitten which had been given to Willie who was married this summer. He ended by saying, "You see, poor Willie was very lonely with nothing but a wife". I suppose he thought the kitten would cheer him up a bit!'

Earlier in the year Mr. Davidson the minister of the United Presbyterian church had left, and there seemed no reason why the U.P. and U.F. churches should not unite in Portree as they had done in the rest of the country. But it was not as easy as one might think. In October mother writes: 'We had a vague intimation from the pulpit today that a congregational meeting would probably be held on the last day of the month to consider union, so things are beginning to move, though slowly. I believe Mr. Macleod would rather leave things as they are, and a good many of his followers are of the same opinion — the less they have to do with the godless U.P.s and their kirk with its kist o' whistles the better'. The U.P. church was carrying on with visiting preachers, and one Sunday mother attended one of their services, taking Allan and me, and found it an improvement on Mr. Macleod. 'They have a young man preaching there, and it was nice to hear a modern sort of sermon and to get back to hymns and music again. I don't think I would have any difficulty in getting Isobel to go there, but she simply hates going to our own. I can manage the others, but she is so strong-willed. Last Sunday I was not going out, and Ronald wanted her to go with him. I tried to get round her by remarking that it was a nice thing for a little girl to take her Daddy to church, but she emphatically replied, "I am not taking Daddy to church. It's Daddy that's taking *me* to church — *much against my will!*"'

No wonder, in the conditions described a week later on the 29th of October. 'I had the two eldest bairns at church, but it was like Greenland as they have not begun to light the stove yet. Not only was the church empty, but poor Mr. Macleod was struggling with a very bad cold. This is the third Sunday he has appeared hoarse as a raven, and what he will be like tonight after standing in that cold church without an overcoat for three services I don't know. Mr. Gillanders tried to make him put off the evening service, but it was no use. "I think he is afraid his people might go to the other church", he told me. So much for the spirit of union!'

At the end of November a meeting took place to discuss the matter. Two church officials had come from Edinburgh with a 'basis of union' expecting to settle things finally, but 'there was strong opposition in the meeting against union at all; a good deal of feeling was shown on both sides, and in the end nothing was settled. I came away very disappointed. Really, Highland congregations are difficult to manage! They hate innovations and will not be driven. Mr. Macleod still had his bad cold today, but the stove was lit, and we would have been comfortable if it had not smelled like Alasdair's penny tin lantern'.

Our religious education at home continued with Sunday Bible Lessons. I reacted strongly against the smug sufficiency of the Wise Virgins. 'Isobel was exercising her Higher Criticism on the Wise Virgins today. "I don't think they were a bit wise, for they fell asleep as well as the others". "Yes", I said, "but they had remembered to take the oil with them". "They should have given some to the others! They were horrid selfish creatures! I hate them!" She was almost weeping because the foolish virgins were shut out'.

And we invented a delightful game which unfortunately could not be allowed. 'The children were having great fun today with what they considered a Sunday game. They have just learned to climb over the garden wall into the graveyard where they pretended they were ghosts. Isobel found a gravestone with Isabella on it, and there is one with Alasdair, so they get behind them and grunt at each other in truly ghostly fashion. I'm afraid I shall have to put a stop to it, as we shall be namely if our children are seen romping in the graveyard.

'Another afternoon when I came home I heard weeping coming from the library and found them all there with the blinds down and the room nearly dark. They were wildly jumping about and trying to frighten Flora by telling her that we were going through the tail of a comet, and if the blinds weren't down it would come in and dreadful things would happen. All of which the poor child firmly believed, and was in great distress. Weren't they monkeys?'

For two years comets had been very much in the news. Halley's comet had been visible from April to June in 1910, and the earth had passed through its tail without anyone except the astronomers noticing it. We must have picked up the phrase then, but our alarming game was suggested by the presence of Brooke's comet, visible from October 22nd to November 4th 1911. I remember seeing from the nursery window its fiery head and long tail glowing over Fingal's Seat. Mother knew that we were only using our imagination for thrills; she probably gave us a mild scolding and comforted Flora, but the poor timid little thing never forgot the terrifying experience.

78

Another epidemic of severe influenza went through the house in December, and kept mother busy with special diets and doctor's visits. However the patients recovered in time to enjoy a Christmas dinner of 'Hare soup, roast goose and pretty puddings.' Among the presents were two books by George MacDonald, *The Princess and the Goblin* and *The Princess and Curdie*, also Barrie's *Peter and Wendy*, which was sent to Alasdair by one of Mr. Alexander Macdonald's sisters. He usually received a well-chosen and much-appreciated book for Christmas because he was the namesake of their dead brother. So the year ends with: 'The children have been playing at pirates, and the crocodile with the clock inside, and the mermaids' lagoon'.

1912: 'Are My Children Quite Normal?'

During January mother read the George MacDonald stories to us in the evenings, and we loved them. 'I have been reading out *The Princess and the Goblins* and enjoying it as much as the children. They listen with *breathless* interest, and Isobel remarked, "I feel the day so long till evening comes and we can have more of the story." I did not know it was quite so good; better, I think, than more modern children's books.' Later I had another exciting literary experience. 'Isobel has been deep in *Treasure Island* today. She read the whole book with keen interest, then said that it was the most thrilling bloody book she had ever read. "The people are just killed in scores." I heard her telling Alasdair. I expect she will start it again tomorrow'.

Then, as now, Portree kept lively during the winter months with classes, lectures, choir practices and small societies. In 1912 there were first-aid lectures, and a series of cookery classes which were not altogether a success. 'Our course of cookery lessons begins tomorrow. I am on the committee, so I expect they will keep me busy. We also have our ambulance lectures once a week; I take Annie out to them. I amuse the children by pretending they are wounded soldiers and practising bandages on them, only I hope I never have Allan for a real patient, for he is so tickly I can't do anything with him. He doubles up and nearly has a fit if I try to find his femoral artery. Annie missed last week's lecture, and I tried to tell her about her circulation and how to stop bleeding. My description must have been too graphic, for she nearly went off in a faint, and had to sit down and take a drink of water. If she could oblige us that way at the class we could have a chance of putting our first-aid into practice'.

A week later in mid-February she writes: 'Our cooking classes have begun and I am sorry to say our new teacher is not a success. She is fully trained, but she is a muddled sort of woman. I have to interview her tomorrow and try to get her to work on better lines. She would have good classes if she could work them properly, but she has no method. She is not young and is very fat and ponderous — 'the white man's burden', Catriona calls her when I bring my woes to her. She was trained by Miss Black's successors, so I feel responsible for her and she looks to me for sympathy and help. Then the oven wouldn't heat properly and the plumber had to be got in to see it, and the woman we got in to assist was drunk and refused to do anything, so she had to be dismissed and another found. So we are labouring under difficulties'.

Next week the news was more cheerful. 'Things have improved all round. The teacher is getting into her work, the oven is heating and the girls turning out well, so I feel in better spirits about it. We are trying to work in the Red Cross Invalid Cookery classes while she is here'.

But their teacher's ideas of invalid cookery and of conducting examinations were not very intelligent. In March we are told, 'Our cookery examination will be merely nominal. Miss P. seems more afraid to ask us questions than we are to answer them, and they are so absurdly simple you couldn't possibly fail. She is going to ask them as she goes along and not all at the end, so, as she has just told us the answer a minute before, we have no time to forget. I nearly broke out into laughter at the last class. She was showing us grilling, and illustrating it with a piece of steak; before she was done, the steak was red-hot and glowing like a cinder. She held it up and asked in an encouraging voice, "Now can any lady tell me where this piece of steak is digested?" We looked blankly at her, so with a bland smile she answered herself, "In the stomach!" If you had seen it you would have said, "Not a human stomach; certainly not an invalid's — perhaps in the stomach of an ostrich'!

Allan, now five, continued to be inquiring and original. 'I think Uncle Allan would be amused at a remark of his namesake which shows that his ideas of applied science are still pretty rudimentary. "Mama, if you looked at a weathercock and found that it stood at blood-heat, would that be a *fearfully* warm day?" On another occasion the problem was moral. "If a man was good all his life, and at the very end he exploded a house, and that was his only sin, would he go to heaven?" This dramatic and spectacular choice of a final sin suited a child who liked to stand out and take the lead. 'You would have been shocked if you had heard a remark of Allan's the other day. He was inquiring after the fate of the ungodly, and Isobel told him frankly that they went to Satan. I wish you had seen the look in his eye as he turned to me with, "Mama, some day Satan will die, and then *I* will be Satan!" He thought that would be a far grander thing than being a mere general, or even an admiral, which has lately been his ambition. He took the funny idea into his head that he had been with the Children of Israel in the wilderness, and that he was Moses. "You needn't give me a Bible lesson on Moses," he said, "for I was Moses myself, and I know all about it" — and then he would tell how he saw the serpents and describe them to me. I sometimes wonder if my children are quite normal. Flora is the only one that seems like other folk'.

Indeed one never knew what Bible lessons might produce. We must have been studying Second Samuel just then, for Alasdair was puzzled over Absalom. 'I told them of his beautiful hair which when cut each year weighed two hundred shekels. This did not convey much to Alasdair, so to get a clearer conception of it he inquired, "How many times would that be of Daddy's?" I found that question beyond me! My imagination was not equal to it, but it would be a long time before Ronald's hair would be a danger to him if he were riding through a wood!' And I was passionately distressed when David poured away the water which his three mighty men had brought him at risk of their lives from the well at Bethlehem. 'When Isobel heard what he did with it her indignation knew no bounds. She threw herself on the floor and wept and cried. "Oh the horrid old thing! Could he not have kept it or done something else with it! He *shouldn't* have poured it out! Oh the horrid old thing!" I think there are many others who share her feelings, though they do not express them so vehemently'.

When we came to Solomon and the choice he made when God asked him to choose any gift — 'Give thy servant therefore an understanding mind to govern thy people, that I may discern between good and evil.' — mother asked us what we would have chosen in like case. 'Under the influence of the lesson Alasdair said he would ask to be good. Isobel would ask to be loved by all, "for that would mean I was good and beautiful and nice." Allan's ambitions ran on no such lines. "I would ask to be a Boy Scout."' He was still too young for such glories, but early in April he went to school for the first time. 'Allan went off to school last Monday, and I believe he has been fearfully good so far; at least, when Alasdair came home on the first day he reported that he was so good "he made me feel ashamed of myself." He is more particular than Alasdair, and does not care about boys who are not tidy and clean. He wouldn't put on a pair of gloves that didn't match in case Miss Robertson might think he was a ragged boy'.

Peter, now two years old, begins to come on the scene. We were all light-haired children, but he had dark hair, cheeks like rosy apples and beautiful dark-blue eyes. He was even slower at learning to speak than Allan had been, but mother did not worry about him; she did not feel so responsible, and by now recognised that children develop at different rates. There is an amusing picture of him with Trionag. 'This week we had a visit from Aunt Catriona and Uncle John from the Glen. They brought wee Catriona with them to see Peter; it was the first time the little brother and sister had met since Peter was three weeks old. At first he was shy, then he was very taken up with her, and was even too attentive, pushing her about and clawing her generally. It was funny to see the three little children together: Peter had no words at all, only gurgles; Catriona only Gaelic and Flora only English. It was a queer chattering, a sort of baby Tower of Babel'.

Church affairs continued to be unsatisfactory. Mr. Macleod at last admitted that his illness was serious and went south to consult a specialist. His place was filled by substitute ministers who were even less inspiring than he was. 'Meanwhile we get some queer specimens. I think George would have enjoyed a story the one we had today told us; his critical mind would have discovered a flaw or two. It was about a lad who was going to sea for the first time. His mother when packing his bag put in a Bible and requested him to read it. Between the pages she slipped a five-pound note. The boy returned; his mother unpacked his bag and found the Bible and the five-pound note untouched. She leaves it there and again asks him to read the Bible. Next voyage the ship is wrecked and the crew cast on a lonely island. Their lives are saved but they lose everything; only this youth had managed to save his mother's Bible (why, when he never read it, he should have troubled, I don't know). While one of the men is reading it they discover the five-pound note, and this through the providence of God was the means of

Ronald and Elizabeth Macdonald with Isobel, Alasdair, Allan and baby Flora.

subsistence to them all. I think George would have asked what they did with the five-pound note if they did not eat it. If there was a Bank of England handy was there not also a Sailors' Rest? Besides, as he would have pointed out, the youth profited not by reading his Bible, but by leaving it unread, which was not the minister's intention'.

Later on, in April: 'Mr. Macleod has three months' leave of absence, and we have a *most tiresome* man here for a month. He is a stickit probationer from Harris: how I am to endure him for three more Sundays I don't know. I had Isobel with me today. She has been a little more reconciled to going to church since she discovered what she always calls "The Revelation of St. John the Divine." It has been a great find to her, and she brings out long sentences from it at unexpected moments'.

In mid-June Annie went off on the Harris boat for two weeks holiday in Staffin, and this time took Flora with her. They came back at the end of the month, and Flora found it difficult to settle into the family again after being everyone's pet in Staffin. 'Flora and Annie came home safely on Friday night, Flora looking fat and rosy and smelling strongly of peat. She has not quite settled down, and complains bitterly and with tears that they were far kinder to her in Staffin than they are here; she got an egg or ham and eggs whenever she wanted it. However she will soon find her place again; we all feel much the same when holidays are over'.

During August our parents took their three older children and Nana to help look after them, to Drumnadrochit, a pleasant village at the end of Glenurquhart near Loch Ness. It was our last family holiday away from Skye. Prosperous Lowland people like mother's family usually rented a house on the Clyde coast for at least a month in the summer, so she had a strong tradition of annual upheaval and settlement elsewhere. But it was always difficult to persuade father to find a suitable place and move away from his natural surroundings with her and some of his children for several weeks. When he had a vacation he preferred to keep Portree as his base and stay for short visits with friends in Inverness or in other parts of Skye. Even on this occasion it was not easy to tear him away from his home, his library and his work. Mother writes soon after our arrival: 'Ronald is never able to make a clean break when he gets his holidays; he does not expect to join us till next Thursday, and even talks darkly of perhaps coming to take us home, but I am hoping that the natural feelings of a husband and father will prove too strong for him, and we shall see him next week at the latest'.

He came. and we all enjoyed every moment of our stay at Drumnadrochit. The village was built round an open green space where Alasdair and Allan joined with some friendly boys who were playing cricket. There was a stream nearby, and a saw-mill where we watched the circular saw shearing into large trees with a tearing scream, and smelled the freshness of pine-sap, and handled sawdust, and found useful pieces of wood to make into boats with Alasdair's birthday box of tools. We specially admired a baby's coffin that was made while we were there; it was covered with sheets of patterned metal foil in black and silver over the bare wood, and we were allowed to pick up and treasure pieces of this adornment. One evening we went to a travelling cinema in a tent, and watched the sinking of the *Titanic* in dim grey on a flickering screen while a wide-horned gramophone played 'Nearer, my God, to Thee'. We scrambled about the ruins of Castle Urquhart on its promontory above Loch Ness, and paddled in clear cold water, and found wild raspberries growing on the hillside and blaeberries heavy with bloomy fruit carpeting a wood. Beside the little steamers that came and went from Temple Pier three primitive motor-coaches connected us with Inverness; they had high rows of seats open to the Highland weather, and their names were written in bold decorative lettering on their rears: the Hare, the Wolf and the Stag. Father read *The Lady of the Lake* to us in the evenings, and I was enchanted by the idea of a girl living on a secret island in Loch Katrine among the mountains; we used to recite together the splendid opening that takes one at the pace of the flying deer deep into the Highlands.

> 'The stag at eve had drunk his fill
> Where danced the moon on Monan's rill;
> And deep his heathery couch had made
> In lone Glenartney's hazel shade.''

And so on. We made a private parody, changing Scott's stag to the Stag motor coach.

Aunt Agnes stayed with us for part of the time, and painted a miniature of my head in water-colours on ivory; it was exhibited later at the Lady Artists' gallery in Blytheswood Square. I wore a smock of very pale soft pink silk, and sat on cushions on the floor against the back of a chair covered in white muslin. To beguile the tedium of the sittings mother read aloud a new book that Aunt Agnes had brought; it was called *The Wind in the Willows*, and I could have listened to it all day.

She went with us on a long excursion by steamer to the Falls of Foyers and the aluminium works; and then down the loch to Fort Augustus and through the Caledonian Canal locks. At Fort Augustus we visited the great church of the Benedictine monastery, and I was enthralled by its solemn beauty — the welcoming figures of the saints; the Stations of the Cross along the walls; the austere dignity of the high altar. I declared that I was going to be a Catholic when I grew up. Mother was amused at another example of her child's oddity, but it was a promise I kept. On another day we visited Inverness and were taken to see Culloden moor and the stone from which the cruel Duke of Cumberland had directed his troops to bring ruin and death to the clans in the cold spring of 1746. Father quoted from Andrew Lang:-

'Dark, dark was the day when we looked on Culloden,
    And chill was the mist-drop that clung to the tree.'

After this solemn sight we drove back to Inverness and had lunch with a wealthy Mr. McEwan who in that northern clime grew peaches and grapes in his greenhouse. These exotic fruits appeared on the table, and we tasted them for the first time with awe and wonder.

We came home at the beginning of September, and Aunt Agnes describes a typical Highland journey. 'The motor-coach should have left Drumnadrochit at eight o'clock, arriving in Inverness at nine-thirty, and our train was at ten o'clock. It was very late in coming; then it went off to a little village to pick up some people. It did not leave till half-past eight, and was so heavily laden that it could only crawl. Before we were near the station in Inverness it broke down altogether — at about four minutes to ten! We had sent the luggage by boat the day before, and were to get it at the station. Lizzie, the children and I rushed off, asking our way as we went, and left Ronald and Nana to see about the luggage. We reached the station at one minute to ten, and of course the train was at a far-away platform. We tumbled into our reserved compartment hot and exhausted, and sat for a solid hour before the train left the station! It was most annoying after our desperate rush, especially with three restless children asking in various tones of complaint, "*When* will the train start?"'

It throws a grim light on motor travel in these days if a motor-coach, however heavily laden, should have taken an hour and a half to cover the distance from Drumnadrochit to Inverness, which cannot be much more than twenty miles. The Highland Railway was notorious as a bad timekeeper, especially on the Dingwall and Skye line, where there was nothing to hurry it, as the steamer had to wait at Kyle till the train arrived.

Soon after we came home my eyes were tested in a routine examination of school-children and found to be defective, so mother took me south for a short visit to have them attended to. When we arrived back in Portree, 'Alasdair and Allan met us, and must have amused the passers-by with their uncontrolled fits of laughter and jeering remarks over poor Isobel's spectacles. However, she took it quite philosophically.' Father had joined us on the boat at Broadford where he had been on business and as soon as he landed he was snapped up by two Bank Inspectors who were entertained to dinner the next evening. Mother proudly encloses her menu.

Nice brown soup.
Boiled fish with French sauce.
Mutton with cauliflower, potatoes and salad.
Grouse with bread sauce.
Apricot tart.
Honeycomb pudding with cream.

'Finishing up with coffee: not bad on such short notice'. I should think not, especially as Julia was still away, and we were making do with a young inexpert cook called Jessie.

The time of Annie's departure was drawing near, as her young mason in Inverness wanted to marry her early in the next year. She had always made a great pet of Allan who was devoted to her and called himself her little husband. While we were at Drumnadrochit he had saved up tenpence by heroic efforts — we were given no regular pocket-money and very little money at any time — which he proudly presented to her when we came home. She bought a belt with it, and Allan became desperate to earn money to support her. 'The only thing he could think of was weeding the garden, and it was both pathetic and amusing to see him out before breakfast, then hurrying back from school at 12.30 and at it again till dinner-time, and again in the evening when the others were playing, all in the vague hope that his Daddy might notice him and give him a penny. Of course I saw that the penny was forthcoming, and it was proudly handed over to the wee wifie. He hopes to earn enough to buy her a dress. I wonder how he will take her departure. We are saying nothing about it as yet, but Isobel asked him the other day, "What would you do if Annie married someone else?" "That wouldn't matter," was the reply, "for he would be dead before I was ready for Annie." "You don't know that," said Isobel. "Yes I do know quite well, for I would kill him," he replied with assurance. So perhaps he will take it calmly in the end. All this devotion makes it very hard for her to go, for she glories in it'.

Granny sent some money as a present for Annie who was delighted. 'She has always had her widowed mother to support, and latterly her sister too, so she has not been able to save much. Our present to her is to be a sewing-machine, and I am going to get a nice work-basket and fit it out from the children'. One wonders how Annie could have saved anything at all from a wage of £20 a year with a mother and sister to support.

She left us at the end of November, and mother was surprised at our lack of feeling. 'I did not know how I was to break it to the children. They knew nothing till the night before she left; then I told them — and what do you think? The little wretches took it quite calmly! Even Allan was interested to hear about her wedding and to know if he would be asked. Then they were taken up with the sewing-machine and work-basket which we presented to her. Only when she went to see Allan after he was in bed was there a bit of a weep. I was concerned about how Peter would take to Maggie as he has very strong likes and dislikes, and Annie a was always his refuge in a time of storm, but there again I have had no trouble; they have been friends from the first. Maggie Mathieson my new girl promises well. She is the eldest daughter of a family of eleven, and has a good father and mother, so she has had a good training and plenty of experience of children. She is very bright and bonny too, and they have all taken to her'.

Indeed Maggie Matheson was a very attractive girl with dark brown hair that curled into little ringlets, and dancing blue eyes. She was livelier than the serious-minded rather nervous Annie who had been so devoted to the three younger children that she was inclined to be impatient with the elder two. Maggie sang Gaelic songs to us and joined in our games, and told us stories about her long family of brothers and sisters and of the tinkers who had a camp near their house up on the moors, and who would come at night and try to steal their peats. There was a gay briskness in the air when she was around that was very much to our taste.

At nine years old I was blessedly innocent and uninstructed. I believed that babies floated down from God into the cradle which I had noticed was usually done up with muslin and put in the spare-room shortly before one arrived. 'Willie the gardener had a little daughter this week, and the week before a baby brother came to her great friend Joanie Ross, so Isobel has been very eager that I should get the cradle ready to see if one wouldn't come here'. And earlier in the year when it was a question of kittens. 'Isobel does not seem to wonder where they came from. Her only remark was, "We thought Tommy was ill when she was mewing so much, but it was just her way of asking God for a kitten."' The idea of babies floating down from the sky to arrive where they were wanted seemed quite reasonable, and if it ever crossed my mind that there might be more to know, I dismissed the matter as a grown-up affair, something I would learn about all in good time, like newspapers and money. I do not remember ever discussing such questions with my friends in Portree school but one night as we curled up together in the nursery bed with the red winter-curtains drawn and firelight dancing on the walls, Alasdair told me all the bad words he had learned from other boys. We took no interest at all in their meaning as we whispered and chuckled; they were merely wicked four-letter noises which we must never make before parents or teachers.

Early in November it was still uncertain where, if at all, church services would be held, and conditions could be very uncomfortable for the persevering few. 'We went to the old U.P. church today, and made a quarter of the congregation of sixteen. It was bitterly cold, especially as the window beside us was broken. The minister was an old man who wore his overcoat, and was nearly lost in its big astrakhan collar. When we make a presentation to our new minister I think it had better be a fur coat rather than a gown and bands for pulpit wear. But the old man gave us a plain homely sermon in a clear voice, and the children came home with frozen toes but quite delighted with him. Isobel especially had listened to every word, and could give a good account to her Daddy when she got home'.

The mention of a new minister indicates that poor old Mr. Macleod had died and the two congregations were at last to be united. When a Scottish church is vacant, ministers who would like to be appointed come to give the congregation a sample of their preaching — a custom that may be embarrassing for both sides. In December mother writes: 'We had our first service as a united congregation today. It was not very well attended, but the cold day would account for that. The preacher was one of the neighbouring ministers who, we hear, is to be a candidate. Catriona and I were wicked enough to smile when he gave out for his text a portion of Isaiah which ended with, "Lord, here I am: send me." He is a decent man and a friend of ours, but a very prosy preacher. I hope he does not expect us to support him, but he very likely does!'

Lady Macdonald stayed at the Lodge till the beginning of November, and mother was called in to help with one of her public-spirited plans. But first there is a description of a children's party where Peter, still speechless and very shy, took a step into high society. The Lodge butler was an impressive grey-haired man who wore a kilt of bright red tartan (he could not have been a Macdonald clansman) and was followed by a woolly dog when he took his walks abroad.

'On Wednesday Lady Macdonald asked me to bring Flora and Peter to a children's party at the Lodge. Her two little grandsons (Mr. Godfrey's children) are staying with her just now. Poor wee Peter has never once had his tea out of the nursery, so it was a big jump for him. He was very good but very awed. He never said a word, and at tea he sat for a long time with his piece in his hand before he had the courage to bite it. He looked very nice in Allan's old white suit with the anchor on it, and white socks. Flora had on her blue silk dress and white socks and beads and ribbon, and was bright and happy, not a bit shy. Little Alasdair, the future Lord Macdonald, is a dear wee boy of three and a half, very musical. He has a tiny set of bagpipes, which of course he can't play, but he marches round the table with them, singing Highland airs quite correctly. One could hardly believe that he was only nine months older than our little Peter who can't say "thank you" yet. After tea the butler played the pipes and all the children marched after him as happily as the children who followed the Pied Piper. It was a pretty sight.

'Her Ladyship's latest idea is to do something for the crowd of boys and girls who attend Portree school as Higher Grade pupils. We have all felt the need of this for some time. There are about ninety pupils from the country who are in lodgings, not always too comfortable. Her idea is to get up a Club for them, so on Thursday we went through torrents of rain to confer on the matter. We have formed a committee of which I am one, but we don't quite know what we are going to do with them all. We have the huge new Drill Hall, but at present no chairs or tables. Lady Macdonald seemed to think we could have it open every night, but that is impossible, so we are going to begin with one night, Saturday.

'Her Ladyship reminds me of a certain nobleman in the Bible who gathered his servants together and said, "Occupy yourselves till I come," and then straightway took his departure. She has given us all our work to do, and then on Tuesday off she goes to London for the winter, and woe betide that wicked and slothful servant who has not made good use of his talents when she returns. The Viewfield and Redcliffe families are going off too, so the work is left to a few of us, none with much leisure. But she is a wonderful woman, so clever, and so kind and good too'.

A week later she describes the opening of the Club which became a lively institution, and must have been of great benefit to the secondary scholars from the Outer Isles and the more remote parts of Skye.

'The first meeting of our Club last night was a great success. We had about sixty boys and girls from thirteen to twenty years old. I went with some fear and trembling, for we did not know very clearly what we were going to do with them, but everything went off very well. We had a piano and gramophone, so after a little music we started games — blind-man's buff, parlour-tig, clubs etc. When we tired ourselves out we had some more music, then went at it again. I don't know when I romped so much. The idea is to give them plenty of fun and exercise, and keep them from wandering aimlessly about the streets as many of them do on Saturday nights. We only managed to get some chairs and benches last night, but next week we hope to have tables. We have three sets of ping-pong and some parlour games, which should make for variety'. Eventually a number of side-lines were introduced: the girls learned to crochet patterns and knit gloves, and some of the boys were taught to play the bagpipes.

Towards the end of November in typical Highland weather of wind and rain father and mother spent a weekend with the Noel Patons in Duisdale House. This large three-storied mansion of grey stone is now a hotel: it stands on the Sound of Sleat near Isle Oronsay with a magnificent view across the strait to the great sombre mountains of Ross-shire. It has a conservatory and a walled garden through which a stream flows; there is a wide lawn in front of the house, and thickets of rhododendron climb up the hillside behind it. Sir Joseph Noel Paton was a popular and prosperous Victorian artist, knighted in 1867. He painted mediæval and allegorical subjects in the style of the minor Pre-Raphaelites with elaborate costumes, bright colours, and an exact rendering of flowers and bramble-sprays and mossy stones in the background. There is one called "The Bluidy Tryst" in Glasgow Art Gallery in which a girl finds her well-dressed lover lying dead, and Edinburgh has an immense picture of Titania and Bottom so swarming with fairies as to suggest a need for fly-spray. His son Ranald who had rented Duisdale House was also a painter, but as he had married a Baird, a daughter of the great iron and steel firm, he would not have to take his art very seriously. She had had an operation and been ordered to avoid all social strain, which explains why they were still in Skye at that dead time of the year.

The picture of post-Edwardian country-house life in the remote Highlands is a delightful one, especially the hymns played on a gramophone in honour of Sunday. An open car of the period was sent to fetch them; 'all the way to Portree, about thirty-four miles,' says mother, amazed at such generosity. They drove by Loch Sligachan with the Cuillins glooming through the mist. 'The car was a Sunbeam and went like a bird. The rain kept off till we were within a few miles of Duisdale, then came down in torrents, so we were glad to reach our destination.

'Duisdale House has had some three or four thousand pounds spent on it, so now it is modern and luxurious. One would fancy from the richness of the carpets, beauty of decoration and perfection of cuisine that one had been transported to London instead of being in the wilds of Skye. Our host and hostess have no children; the only other member of the household was a nephew of Mrs Paton's, a tall young guardsman. Her mother was one of the famous Bairds, so their chief concern in life is *not* to keep the wolf from the door'.

They arrived in time for afternoon tea on Saturday, then chatted till it was time to dress for dinner. It would be interesting to know what mother changed into, but she hardly ever mentions clothes, and only says casually that she was glad she had her 'altered' dress, though it was much the same as the one their hostess had worn during the afternoon, and came far short of the 'gold satin trimmed with Brussels lace' in which Mrs Paton appeared at the dinner table. There would be candles in silver candlesticks with red shades, and flowers from the conservatory in crystal vases, and six or seven courses of delicious food; then they went back to the drawing-room and had music from a very fine gramophone. On the following morning 'the rain came down in sheets, and as the nearest church was some eight miles away we could not go to service. Later the rain cleared off and we had a walk, and read and talked and heard hymns on the gramophone for the rest of the day'.

They left early on the Monday morning as father had to be back at business in Portree, and the journey through the Cuillins was quite an adventure.

'They sent us back in the motor. It was wet as usual, but they lent us oilskins and sou'westers and put a hot-water bottle at my feet, so we were quite comfortable. But we had a wild time coming home; every now and then there would be a fierce gust of wind and driving hail and sleet, and as we were going at a good rate it stung our faces till we felt that a little more would take the skin off. The road too is wild and grand, winding among those awesome hills with the storm-clouds rolling round their heads. It certainly was an experience, but one I enjoyed on the whole'.

At the beginning of December our dear Julia came back to us. For some reason she was staying at Applecross which has always been one of the most difficult places to reach in the whole of Wester Ross, and she had an atrocious journey back to Raasay before crossing to Portree. 'I gave her a few days so that she might go home before coming here. Applecross is just opposite to Raasay, her home, but as there is no direct communication and the weather was too stormy to cross in a small boat, she had to go to Stornoway, stay a night there, then go to Kyle of Lochalsh and from there to Raasay where she had to stay another night before she could walk to her home — a journey of three days and two nights to reach a place she could see! And poor Julia is a wretched sailor, and hates the sea'.

It seems strange that she could not have joined the *Sheila* on its inward voyage in the early morning, and changed to the Portree steamer at Kyle instead of voyaging to Lewis and back again. But Applecross had no pier and was served by a ferry-boat: in December the day might be so dark and the weather so stormy that the steamer would not risk stopping to take on passengers. Faced with the prospect of going out in the pitch-black morning hours on a tossing ferry-boat to await in seasick misery the arrival of a steamer which might sail past with a melancholy blast from its siren, poor Julia preferred to travel by daylight, even though it meant a longer voyage.

And before she arrived there was a domestic disaster — the back part of our house which contained the main water supply was old and the pipes often gave trouble. 'On Tuesday morning when I got up I found water pouring through the bathroom and lobby ceilings. You never saw such a flood! The water was so deep on the landing that the children were gaily sailing their toy boats on it, and it was pouring down the stairs to the floor beneath. Would you believe it? — the girls never thought of running for the plumber, and never wakened me a minute earlier to see what was to be done, but just let it pour! I couldn't remember where the tap was to turn off the water for the house, but I made my way through it in my bedroom slippers and rushed up to the garret where I found the escape pipe from the tank gushing out water. The only thing I could think of was to tie Ronald's pyjamas round it till the plumber came, which he did remarkably quickly for him. Then after breakfast, just as Ronald was going into the bathroom, down came the ceiling, fortunately not on his poor unprotected head, but it was a narrow escape. We have kept big fires in the pink room and nursery ever since, but the walls and ceilings are still damp'.

There were other difficulties in Portree during the winter. Eggs and milk and fish were often very scarce, and in mid-December of this year Mr. Mackinnon the village baker died — he was the grandfather of my friend Nanette Macrae — and his shop was closed for almost a week. 'We managed to get Glasgow bread in the shops till yesterday when it gave out. The usual Saturday Glasgow boat did not come, so there is not a loaf in the place. The milk is very scarce this winter too; many a family has to do with a pint a day, and happy to get as much. The eggs were so scarce all summer that though I preserved as many as I could we had to be constantly using them, and they are now finished'.

During the Christmas season the family was again laid low with influenza and bronchitis. Mother surveys her ailing brood. 'I can never have the pleasure of nursing one invalid at a time; as soon as one falls ill the rest follow. They are all barking like a pack of dogs today, and lying in front of the fire, so after dinner I packed them off to bed. I was thankful to get rid of them'. The Christmas holidays must have been rather dismal, but we were ready for school again early in January.

1913: Quarantine Spring And Glenhinisdale Summer

Early in the year there is a glimpse of Annie's wedding, a pleasanter and less strenuous affair than the January wedding in Raasay at which she was best maid in 1908. It took place at the Temperance Hotel in Kyle of Lochalsh where the bride's party arrived from Skye by boat and the bridegroom's from Inverness by train, and after a happy celebration parted for their homes in the evening. None of the family was there, so Allan did not see Annie's union with the hated rival, but both Julia and Nana were present since Atten came to us with her maid, setting them free to enjoy a whole day's outing.

Then mother comments on her bonnie little Peter who was at last beginning, slowly and hesitatingly, to put words together, and to say 'Mama's!' when she put her arms round him and asked 'Whose boy are you?' and she adds, 'It was wonderful how little the children missed Annie. When anything went against Peter he used to go to the door and sob piteously for "Wee Annie! Wee Annie!" but the others took her departure very calmly, even Allan. I have been very fortunate in Maggie. She is old-fashioned and motherly for her age — she is only twenty — and yet she is bright and plays with the children more than Annie did. The darning may suffer in consequence, but one can't have everything, and I think I prefer to have the children kept happy'. It may be a sad truth, but little children do not mourn the departure of one kind person for very long if another kind person comes in her place.

As well as being rigid Sabbatarians the Free Presbyterians frowned on most forms of secular entertainment. Their idea of virtue was to sit quietly at home reading the Bible and meditating on Death and Judgement, and they did not approve of putting temptation in other people's way. As far as possible they suppressed story-telling, dancing and Gaelic songs, so that Mrs Kennedy Fraser found very little material for her great collection in the Isle of Skye. Mother tells the sad story of an attempt to have some gaiety in Braes, a beautiful scattered community which lies along the shore of Raasay Sound between the south end of Ben Tianavaig and Loch Sligachan.

'I must tell you about the fate of a concert which was to be held at a little place called Braes. It will show you how far back we still are here in appreciation of the arts and graces of life. It was proposed by the schoolmaster to have a sort of afternoon soirée for the children — a bun and cup of tea affair. Then in the evening to have a concert, the proceeds of which were to pay for the children's entertainment, and if anything was over it was to go to provide cocoa for the children's lunch. Could anything be more innocent or more laudable? The school is under the Portree School Board, so they applied to Ronald as Clerk for permission to have it there. He sent a letter round the members, and they all seemed to agree except Mr. MacRae the Free Presbyterian minister, so he wrote granting permission. When Mr. MacRae heard of this he was very annoyed, for most of the Braes folk belong to his congregation. He made Ronald call a meeting of the school board: only four members turned up, but one of them was one of his own elders. The voting was two against two, but Mr. MacRae was chairman, so he used his casting vote and carried his point. When Ronald pointed out that permission had been given and expenses already incurred Mr. MacRae offered to pay £1 to defray the expense, but insisted that the concert be stopped. So there was nothing for it but to write refusing permission to use the school for such ungodly purposes. I think his idea was that *he* uses the school for services when he goes there to preach, and it would be a terrible thing to have people laugh at a comic song in the same building. It did seem a pity, as an entertainment of any kind is a very rare event in Braes'.

At that time I lived two lives: one of ordinary home and school, and the other pervaded with poetry. I read all I could find; I wrote it, without much originality, but with the greatest delight in finding rhyme-words and simple metre-shapes to contain my moments of joy, and I moved in the company of fairies, mermaids, giants and goblins, by the shore, in the wood, or among the hazel trees and rising steeps above the bay. The two lives were equally vivid. I do not think I visualised these imaginary beings; they were presences rather than faces, as Susie had been when I was four, but I was intensely aware of the sea-spirits who came ashore in the breaking waves on moonlit nights, or the wicked enchanter who swept across the bay on rain-clouds and brooded over the rock-castle where I had once found a dead raven hanging in a trap. I had never been teased or mocked at home about my other life; my family accepted it with quiet sympathy as my special thing. So, as I was fond of my friends at school, I wanted to show them my enchanted places and share their delights, with no idea that they would disbelieve, or that there could be any conflict. The sceptic probably meant to tease rather than to be deliberately unkind, but the smart of her unbelief and the insult to the imaginary presences whom I loved was agonising.

'Poor Isobel has been having troubles. For the last fortnight we have heard about a wonderful "secret place" she has in the wood. I saw it from a distance, and a more dreary desolate spot you could not imagine, but to her it is a fairyland of delight; she visits it every day and comes home raving about it. Every part of it is fantastically named, and inhabited by all sorts of elfin beings. In her innocence she shared her secret with her companions and took them to see it. Most of them were sympathetic but among them was one not clothed in the wedding-garment of romance who made game of her and tore the moss from the fairy houses and the precious fungi from the trees. Isobel came home weeping bitterly. I advised her to go by herself and never mind the girls. So she and Alasdair who is a loyal adherent set off after school, but they were followed by the mischief-maker who again mocked her and committed sacrilege in her sacred places, and again she came home in tears. She was so upset and her eyes so sore with weeping that she could scarcely do her lessons. But next day she came home radiant. The girls had said they were sorry and kissed her, and then there had been a great reconciliation, and they all danced in a ring to show they were friends. Poor little thing! a glint of sunshine one morning sent her dancing up to school with all her nerves tingling, throwing her bag into the air and catching it again. As soon as she had a free moment she must write a poem on spring. "The words just came *tumbling* out of my pencil," she told me'.

Towards the end of February Flora developed scarlet fever, which at that time could be a serious illness with damaging complications, though nowadays one seldom hears of it; the germ must have either died out or become much less virulent. As well as being potentially dangerous it was considered very infectious; the patient had to be strictly isolated for six weeks, either at home or in hospital, and if at home, her family must stay in quarantine until she had recovered; there could be no question of the other children going to school. Flora was put into the spare-room and a motherly woman was engaged to look after her. The Sanitary Inspector came 'with his mysteries and bad smells' to disinfect the nursery, and mother hoped there would be no more cases in the household. 'I am doing my best to keep them away from infection, but what can you do with an imp of a boy like Allan who out of pure devilry rolled himself up in a shawl Flora had used "just to see what would happen. Nothing has happened so far, but my heart jumps every time one of them sneezes'.

We enjoyed Flora's scarlet fever very much, and as she had a mild attack it was not too unpleasant for the patient. Comfortably isolated in the spare-room she had the undivided attention of her kindly nurse who had ingenious ways of keeping a small child amused. Every morning when she had finished her breakfast-egg she was given her paint-box to decorate the empty shell; then it was admired and added to a row on the mantelpiece. She could hear us playing on the landing and shouting to each other from the nurseries, and though we couldn't see her we could call through the door shrouded with its carbolic sheet.

During the mild days of early spring we played for long mornings by the sea on the rocky shores of the Lump where green points were opening on honey-suckle vines and celandines glittered among the wet leaves. We crept into dens barely child-size; we scrambled down to ledges and claimed them as discovered territory. Alasdair had a bower in a hollow where a thick ivy-bush grew from a scarp. We collected cones and piled up seaweed for undefined compelling purposes. For six weeks we were free to hear the seagulls and smell pine-needles and salt water, and see the sunlight come and go on the hills around Portree bay.

In mid-March the weather was broken, but we continued to have a delightful time. 'The children have taken possession of an old meat-safe in the garden and converted it into a house. I found the three of them curled up inside and the rain pouring outside; they seem to find far more amusement within its walls than in their cosy nursery. They have nailed up a board with "Private" painted on it, and decorated the inside with pictures, and there you are — what more do you want? — a biscuit-tin to sit on, and a jam-jar with Christmas roses in it for adornment. They are enjoying their freedom and won't have a decent rag to wear at the end of it. Alasdair came to me with a fearful tear down the front of his trousers, and where do you think he got it? On the douche above the bath! He and Allan were climbing up the back and down the front, so I had to cut out new ones then and there, for they were the best he had'.

At the end of March Flora came back to us again; the nurse left and the Sanitary Inspector performed another thorough fumigation. Mother now felt that to have five children between nine and three years old rushing about the house in a state of boundless energy could be exhausting: since West Highland weather made us spend a good deal of time indoors we needed some place of our own where our games and interests could have more scope than in the nurseries which had to be kept tidy, and where the floor-space was limited by a large bed in each. On the third storey of the old house there was a big lumber-room crammed with accumulated trash — 'bundles of old magazines; huge boxes of legal documents, school-books of people long dead, and our own rubbish of the last thirteen years'. All this was cleared out, and the attic was made into a delightful play-room for us. The maids got interested and offered to whitewash the ceiling and paper the walls themselves. 'I have bought some cheerful paper with bunches of pink roses. We shall remove the dolls' village there, and Prince Charlie the rocking-horse, and the children will be able to make a good deal of mess without always being told to tidy up'.

Spring inspires poets, but in my case composition was carried on under difficulties. 'The first bright day awoke Isobel's muse, which has been asleep for some weeks, and she set off with a doll in one hand and a pencil and a sheet of paper in the other down to the shore at the Lump. At dinner-time she came back with a very limp half-sheet of paper with some verses on The Sea written on it. It should have had another verse, but she broke the point of her pencil, and the paper fell into a pool, and the boys came and tormented her. I suggested she might finish it next day; she did start off with more paper and two pencils stuck inside her stockings for want of a pocket, but as I thought, she never could recapture the first fine careless rapture'.

But there were other more social activities in which I could join. 'The wee laddies of the place have formed themselves into a band of "Boy Scouts" and amuse people by marching about with paper hats and wooden swords and a banner and any amount of side. They are led by Neil Mackinnon who has a real helmet and uniform. Alasdair and Allan are with them heart and soul, Allan wearing Alasdair's old reefer coat with brass buttons as the nearest thing he can get to a uniform. Yesterday Isobel was marching at their tail, hatless and coatless, with a box of dressings under her arm as an army nurse.

Then they had a great battle at the Lump, and she had to attend to the wounded. They have their rules and regulations; they must all salute every lady they meet, and if anyone swears (the oldest of them will be nine or ten) he has a tumbler of cold water poured down his neck. So I think it is a movement to be encouraged'.

Spring cleaning was again in full swing, and this year it was more than usually trying. The library with its several thousand books was a Herculean task, and a fickle chimney-sweep can ruin a carefully planned operation. And there was always the Skye weather! 'I have been driven nearly distracted by my spring cleaning! The first days were wet nearly all the time, with short spells of sunshine which induced you to put out chairs and carpets, followed by deluges of rain which forced you to fly and rescue them. Willie was as cross as a bear. The only place where he thinks he can beat carpets is the top of the Lump, and it is no joke to carry our heavy carpets up and down there. Then I wanted the library chimney swept; it had to be done before we could attack the wearisome books. I arranged for a man to come before breakfast on Tuesday; he comes to see me on Monday half-drunk. "How can he come to me when he hasn't been to the places he should have done today?" I am not sure whether he is coming or not, but have everything ready on the chance. Tuesday morning; no man. I go to his house after breakfast and find he is in bed "ill"! The man who works with him can't come because he has left his working clothes in Raasay. I suggest he might get the loan of the other man's clothes. Perhaps he might; they will send for him. About eleven o'clock a dapper young man with a collar and tie appears and looks up at the chimney. It is wet and stormy, but he is obliging and says he will try it, but he must go home and "shift his clothes." When he come back he finds that his ladder is at the Lodge and must be fetched. About twelve he arrives with it: it is too short: he must go for another. Finally about one o'clock the chimney does get swept, but meantime I have two worried maids and a charwoman who can't get on, and a painter is coming at ten next morning, and all the books must be done and the paint washed before this. We had to work like demons to get it done, but we managed it'.

Peter was an active inquisitive little boy who needed constant watching. 'On Thursday we had one of the proprietors of Raasay to dinner, which meant a busy morning in the kitchen preparing sweets and savouries. I usually have Flora and Peter dancing attendance, and it is not easy to keep an eye on their restless energies. You can imagine my horror when by the merest chance I saw Peter busily engaged in shaking knife-powder out of a tin into the coffee-grinder! As the knife-powder is exactly like ground coffee, had I not happened to notice him it would never have been seen, and we would all have wondered what could be wrong with the coffee. It is wonderful what mischief a small child can do without meaning it. Yesterday I saw him playing with the key of a cupboard in the pantry in which all sorts of necessary stores are kept; in a moment the key had disappeared; it just vanished. At last we got it out of him that he had locked the door and then squeezed the key through a small disused keyhole beside the right one. Of course we at once wanted all sorts of things out of the cupboard. All the keys in the house were tried in vain. Willie had to be sent to the joiner's for more keys, and at last, after much delay and inconvenience, the cupboard was opened, and there was the key inside'.

In July Allan also caused a good deal of trouble without meaning it. He and Alasdair shared a bed, but as they were inclined to riot about in the nursery instead of settling down, Allan was put into our parents' bed to begin with, and carried down fast asleep by Nana at ten o'clock when she came to prepare the room for the night. One evening she found the door locked on the inside. 'She came for me, and we both thumped on the door and shouted, but with no effect. Then Ronald came, and the three of us thumped and shouted and shook the door; still dead silence from the other side. I brought the dinner-bell and rang it; no effect. Then I rang it and we all thumped and called at the same time; not a movement from the other side. At first we were in fits of laughter, then we began to be alarmed. It seemed that no human being could sleep through the din we had been making, and I had visions of Allan locking the door and then exploring the press where I kept my physic bottles. By this time it was after ten and a wet night, but there was nothing for it but to send for Willie, and for Willie to hunt for a ladder and climb through the window. When he opened the door we found the young rascal sleeping the sleep of innocence. I have lost faith in the hymn that talks of "infants' slumbers pure and light." They may be pure, but they are anything but light. He was carried downstairs without waking, and knew nothing about it in the morning. His explanation was that *he thought he heard a noise*, and was frightened, so he locked the door! If he heard noises that had no existence he was deaf enough to those we made!'

This year our parents solved the problem of our summer holidays by sending all the children to Glenhinisdale with Maggie for the month of August, while they enjoyed two weeks of blissful calm at home before joining us. When father and his brothers had become prosperous they had contributed to the rebuilding of the primitive cot where they had been born, and it was now a substantial stone house with two stories, five bedrooms, a kitchen, a sitting-room and a pleasant glazed-in sun-porch in front, though with no bathroom or indoor water-supply. Water for washing and cooking came from the brook that flowed past the house, and drinking-water from a moorland spring. Two of the bedrooms contained two large double beds each, but it must have been a tight squeeze to fit everyone in. The original inhabitants of the house were Grannie, Uncle John, Aunt Catriona, Cousin Peter John, Aunt Jessie's son, a boy in his early teens who had been sent to Skye from Glasgow after an illness, and Trionag aged five, sister of our little Peter. To these were added five more children and a maid, and eventually father and mother. We were very much on top of each other, especially in wet weather.

Glenhinisdale was beautiful but bare; I missed the woods and the sea. But there was a fine salmon-river, and a noble line of hills closed in the head of the glen. We were free to roam and climb and scramble wherever we liked, barefoot and in our oldest clothes. No one ever said the word danger to us, though I had one alarming experience when I tried to wade across the river after heavy rain on one of my solitary rambles and was almost swept away. There was no rigidity about meals; if we missed one we could stay our stomachs with a scone and Auntie's good butter till the next came to the table. Uncle John would take two or three of us astride on Darkie the mare up the hillside for peats; our bare legs felt the strong muscles moving under her satin skin, and on the way back when the pannier-creels were filled we would run alongside on our hardened feet through the heather and bog-myrtle. We collected eggs, and carried drinking-water from the spring, and in the cool Highland gloaming we helped to round up the cows, smacking them with stalks of yellow ragwort, and driving them to the gate where the calves waited hungrily. It was opened; they ran to their mothers to suck on one side while Auntie and Maggie milked on the other, crooning softly and brushing away the midges. The landscape was ours; waterfalls in deep clefts; caves among the rocks; islands in the river: we could pass from play to story-telling and thence to the moments of vision that Wordsworth knew, when the streams have voices, and the hills brood over the glen, solemn and aware.

At home in early August mother was enjoying more tranquillity than she had known at any time for the last nine years, and this heavenly calm was especially marked on Sunday. 'Today has been a real day of rest and gladness. No noisy and reluctant children to worry into Sunday clothes and shoo to church, to keep employed during the afternoon hours; to feed and duly instruct. Instead to have a leisurely breakfast; read a little; walk out coolly and calmly to church; return to a quiet and orderly house; sit down comfortably with a book, and only rise to enjoy a tempting and peaceful meal. Could anything be more delightful, or a greater contrast to the usual hurly-burly of Sunday?'

Communion came round again next week, and Grannie arrived in Portree for the services. As the weather was unusually fine these were held in the open air. 'I can see them through the window as I write, and the slow wail of the psalms and impassioned eloquence of the preacher are wafted quite distinctly across the fields. The midges have been perfectly diabolical lately, and I expect that, large as the congregation is, they will form a much larger one. I was wondering if they might serve a useful end by shortening the service a little, but I expect their victims have too much of the blood of the martyrs in them, and would rather sit and have it sucked drop by drop than shorten their devotions by five minutes. I have said, dinner at four-thirty; I wonder if they will be home by then. They began at eleven, but I have seen them go on till five. Grannie seems very well this time. Sometimes I can get her to miss a service, but this time nothing will induce her to miss even an English one, so she has been more in **the church** than in the house since she came'.

After the two peaceful weeks mother was beginning to miss her children. Grannie brought news, but at first it was rather frustrating. 'Grannie had lots of stories about them which she poured out to Ronald *in Gaelic*, so that all

I could make out was their names, and neither would stop for a moment to explain! However I did learn subsequently that they are all very well, and according to Grannie, remarkably good children. They have had lovely weather and have been out of doors all the time, barefoot and bare-headed. Alasdair goes with Uncle John and helps him with the peats and the work of the farm; Isobel goes exploring and has all sorts of named varieties of kingdoms and islands. The wee ones go about with Grannie after the ducks and hens. Peter has an occupation that keeps him busy and happy for a long time; he gets an old ladle and tries to empty the burn with it!'

So in mid-August they joined us, and mother gave us much-needed baths in a long peat-brown pool. I remember the brightness of the water; the silky feel of its flow in my long hair, and its voice as it curved to the pool in a shallow fall. Bushes of heather grew among the grey rocks; I could float in the stream and bury my face in warm honey-scented flowers. 'I have just been down at the river giving them all a bath. A perfectly beautiful day, warm and clear and bright; the river sparkling in the sunshine; the great hills around us; the sky a cloudless blue; six little naked bodies splashing in a big pool, and Mama with her skirts up and bare feet taking them one by one and giving them a good lathering with soap and a large sponge, while further up the river Daddy might be seen swimming in a still larger pool. After the bath a biscuit, then Daddy and the older ones go off to help in the hayfield while I take the wee ones home and change Flora who sat down in the river by mistake after putting her clothes on'.

Then there is a description of life in a Highland small-holding. 'Everyone is busy here. John is sometimes up at three in the morning to look after the lambs who have just been taken from their mothers; once he was up all night with them. Catriona had fresh butter made before breakfast this morning. Tomorrow they are to be up early and light a fire under a big pot near the burn to get a washing done. It is not easy to cook for thirteen people on an open peat fire, but it is wonderful what can be done. I thought at first I could never work with such a fire, but I am getting quite used to it, and used too to the flavour of peat smoke which it is impossible to avoid'.

It was a beautiful summer, and father and mother helped with the hay-making till their unaccustomed muscles ached all over, but inevitably rain came at last. 'If the sun had continued to shine we would have been crippled for life, but we woke on Thursday to find the hills shrouded in mist and rain coming down steadily, making useless all our work of spreading and turning the hay the day before. At first we enjoyed the enforced rest and leisure, but when the rain continued all Friday and with brief intervals all Saturday, I found my thoughts turning to the comforts of the National Bank House with its library and fire of English coal, its kitchen range and bathroom, and its convenient nursery and play-room where inconvenient children could be banished out of sight. Six little children are one thing roaming about a farm barefooted in warm weather, but quite another thing shut up in a farmhouse on a wet cold day. They begin the day barefoot and look cold; you order them to put on shoes and stockings. Next thing they have all run out and come in with soaking feet. More stockings have to be found; before long these are wet too, and the day ends as it has begun, with bare feet, only there is a long row of socks and stockings hanging on a string across the kitchen fireplace getting permeated with peat-smoke.

'Peter John the thirteen-year-old cousin is a great fisher, and has brought home some salmon-trout of about one and a half or one and three-quarter pounds which has been a welcome change in our diet. The way he catches them is very clever. Sometimes he uses his rod in the ordinary way, but sometimes he sees the salmon in a pool, takes off his clothes and quietly creeps in beside it. Often he has only his mouth above the water. He tickles the salmon, beginning at its tail and gradually working up till he gets to the gills when he quickly slips in his finger and hooks it. He says it likes being tickled and lies quite still. He has caught some big fish in this way'.

The fine weather came back next week, and our different pastimes are described. 'Isobel wanders away by herself, and is perfectly happy climbing to the tops of the hills, tracing the burns to their sources, eating blaeberries and crowberries and finding white heather. The hills across the river are her land of romance and adventure. There live her fairies and dragons, elves and gnomes, and she spends happy hours among them. She is writing a story but makes slow progress. "I cannot write here," she says, "but I am gathering a lot of material."

'Alasdair is sometimes away the whole day with Uncle John, watching the sheep-dipping or fetching stores with the horse and cart from Uig. At other times he goes fishing with Peter John, and they forget all about time and dinner. They came home yesterday with three dozen small trout at five o'clock. I asked if he was hungry. "Yes: is it nearly *dinner-time?*" he replied.

'Allan likes to stay with the wee ones, and leads them into all sorts of mischief such as chasing the ducks down the waterfall or scaring the hens. There is a big bull in the Glen which fascinates him. He is afraid of it, yet can't help stalking and watching it. The same bull is on friendly terms with our cows at present, and turns up when they are milked. I was terrified at first, but am now getting used to doing my small milking with its eyes on my back, though a Highland bull is a fearsome object even at a distance.

'Flora and Trionag are great friends and inseparable. Peter is rather out of it. He and his wee sister quarrel a good deal, the only two who do. On fine days we hardly see the children except at meals, and perhaps not even then. They have hardly had a stocking on all the time: during our last year's holiday at Drumnadrochit Nana seemed to spend her whole time darning stockings. At bedtime there is a pail of water put down by the kitchen fire and they all wash their feet and legs.

'But farming in this climate is a difficult business! The hay which was cut a fortnight ago is still lying in the fields. When a good day comes we turn it and work at it, but the next day is wet and all our work has to be done over again; two good days would finish the whole thing. Then perhaps it is arranged to dip the sheep on a certain day, but in the morning the hills are covered with mist and it is impossible to gather them. So it goes on; the weather constantly interfering with the arrangements for work. Today is a splendid working day, but then it is Sunday! We could have finished the hay; tomorrow as likely as not we shall not be able to touch it'.

This glorious holiday lasted well into September, since alterations were being made in Portree school which could not open till they were completed. During the last week the sun shone and a north wind blew, which sharpens colour in the Highlands and gives distances an unusual clarity. Rowan berries glow scarlet, and heather is a strong deep purple under the cloudless sky. Maggie went off for her holiday and Julia took her place; then came the last day, and a large motor was ordered to take the whole party home.

'It was to be at the Glen at three o'clock and at that hour we had all the boxes taken over the burn, all the children washed and clad in unaccustomed shoes, stockings, collars and other etceteras of civilisation, but no motor came! The weary minutes passed, one of us after another walking up the road as if thinking to bring it more quickly by doing so, but at last we felt sure that our order had been forgotten and it would not come. Ronald went to help with the final haystack; Julia started to bake scones as there was no bread in the house, and we all felt rather ruffled at the thought of unpacking and settling down for another weekend. Then, about six o'clock, the motor arrived. It had been sent out with a party, and the fine day tempted them to keep it longer than they should have done. We were all thankful to see it; it was such an easy way to get home, to step into a motor with your luggage at one door and in an hour and a half to step out at the other door instead of the long tiresome journeys we have had in former years'. Nowadays an hour and a half would be considered rather slow for the fifteen miles between Portree and Glenhinisdale.

Aunt Agnes came to stay, and in writing to arrange the visit mother mentioned a 'small operation' that Flora was going to have. This was a tonsillectomy performed in barbarous fashion by the young doctor without any anæsthetic. The child, sitting on mother's knee, was told to show the doctor her throat. When she opened her trusting little mouth he attacked. She was only five years old, but all her life she remembered the shock and blood and pain; mother would never have allowed it if she had known what it would be like. Our play in the garden was arrested in horror when we heard her anguished screams coming from the nursery window.

Mother went south with her sister and stayed away for some weeks, coming home to find her family rather neglected. 'I was greeted with cries of "I was away from school all week with a cold!" "I was absent two days with a headache!" "I had a sore leg!" Indeed I thought they were all rather pale, and it was time their mother came home to look after them. I have been dosing them with Parish's syrup and tidying them up generally. Not one nail had been cut since I left home, so they all looked like young Nebuchadnezzars with nails like birds' claws.

'Peter is the one satisfactory child I have. He is the picture of health, and has been making me laugh by describing his own creation. "God made me of plasticene with his own knife; he put on my skin with nails and a hammer, then he told me to go home."'

The new minister, Mr. Morrison, had started a Sunday school in connection with the U.F. church, and mother breathed sighs of relief as she sent off four of her five children instead of instructing them herself. 'I have only Peter at home, and he entertains me with stories and extraordinary statements such as, "I was sitting on God's knee last night," or "I was on top of the church roof. God held a ladder for me and I got up, and then God watched me from the garden." He seems to be on very intimate terms with his Maker at present'.

In November Julia left us to get married, with many regrets at the parting. Mary the new cook was much less of a personality. She was given a pretty teaset by the parents and a case of teaspoons by the children. In December the travelling dentist arrived in Portree; he had made an earlier visit in March when we were all in quarantine, and had dealt with the school-children in comprehensive and summary style. 'The poor wee things were driven down like sheep in batches of a dozen or so, without Mamas or nurses, and had their teeth howked out. In the two and a half days he howked out about two hundred teeth from seventy children. He told Ronald he had never seen such bad septic mouths in any place'. This time poor Alasdair was one of the victims. 'Alasdair had four back teeth taken out all at once. He was quite cheery through it all, and smiled up at me between each. Two of the teeth had abscesses, but the dentist seemed able to take them out almost painlessly. However when he went to bed his gums were very sore, and he had a good cry before he finally went to sleep. Nana also visited the dentist and had all her upper teeth taken out; she also had a bad night afterwards and a very swollen face for some days, but she has been able to do her work in a shawl-round-the-head kind of way'.

Alasdair now aged eight was a generous-hearted little boy: when Christmas approached and another beautiful book arrived for him from Mrs Mackinnon mother wrote: 'I am pleased that he gets this little extra bit of Christmas, for he has such a way of giving away his possessions that he never has anything for himself. Cousin Charlie sends him a bundle of cigarette-cards, and by the time he writes his thanks-for-all-your-kindness letters he has not one to bless himself with, and yet he is just as grateful as if he had them all. He thinks Isobel would like the flowers and Allan the coats of arms, so he gives them all away'.

Christmas brought another remarkable present; the first gramophone we had ever heard. Alasdair had been isolated on a false alarm of scarlet fever, but he was able to share the rapture it brought to the whole household. Mother writes to her family who gave it: 'I had no idea I would like it so much, and the children are crazy about it. I wish you had seen their faces on Christmas day when we had our first concert. Then poor Alasdair wanted to have his share, so I took it down to his room and left the door open, and the maids and children gathered on the landing, and we had all the tunes over again, and it was just delightful'.

Father's friend Mr. Thomson of Eigg and Strathaird died just before Christmas, and his romantic choice of burying-place caused trouble in the December storms. 'It was a funeral Ronald is not likely to forget. Mr. Thomson was buried on a small island off the coast of Eigg; he himself had had it prepared, and had bought his own coffin some years ago. It was a wild wet day, and they had difficulty in landing and in getting the remains to the place of burial. The wind and the rain and the wild waves dashing round the island made it very impressive.'

And the year ends with an account of our Christmas dinner. 'A grateful client sends us a goose every Christmas, and each year it is tougher than the previous one. I have learned by experience to pay particular attention to the adjuncts such as stuffing, sausages and bread sauce, so that we may be practically independent of the main dish. When it is preceded by kidney soup and followed by plum pudding, jellies and fruits, we can afford to let it play the role of the ornamental'.

1914: 'He Might Not Come Home Again For Months'

As Alasdair showed no signs of peeling he was allowed to rejoin his family early in January. But meanwhile there had been an accident to the new gramophone on which we doted so absorbedly. 'The evening after Christmas the children had all got chairs outside Alasdair's room and we were going to have a grand concert, but as I was winding it up for the first time the spring snapped! Oh what a change in the happy expectant faces! What weeping and wailing! "Get a joiner to mend it! Get a joiner to mend it!" cried Peter. However I find that half-a-crown will put it right, but a part of it had to be sent back to the shop, so that we haven't had it to enliven the holidays, which was a keen disappointment to us all after we had once heard it. Tomorrow night we expect it back, and we are looking forward to its arrival as if it were a near relation'.

When it came back it was played every evening; we could not have too much of it. Father was as interested as any of us, and brought back records of Gaelic songs and of pipe and drum bands when he went to Inverness on business. Mother went in for violin solos of Mendelssohn's *Spring Song* and of *Angels Guard Thee*, there were overtures to *Zampa* and *The Poet and Peasant*, and among the original records sent with the gramophone was one with *How do you do, Miss Ragtime?* on the one side and *On the Mississippi* on the other, which father deplored as vulgar, but which we dearly loved. So we had plenty of variety, though even then records of really great music were available, and our musical perception might have been developed, as our literary sense grew from the books we found in father's library. But grown-ups as well as children were musically naive in these early gramophone days; simply to hear a tune repeated till one knew every phrase and variation was pleasure enough. 'Each child has adopted a tune of his own, just as we used to have our own Clyde steamers, and you find out to which child any tune belongs by watching their faces while it is played. If I were a photographer I would have a gramophone on the premises. There is nothing like it for keeping a group of children quiet, and all with seraphic expressions on their faces'.

A new sheriff, Sheriff Boswell, had come to Portree with an unmarried sister to keep house for him. They were lively interesting people, especially Miss Boswell, who wrote plays and produced them with the children of the Episcopal church to which she belonged. We had so few outings that an amateur play or an evening at the Club were as exciting as a circus or a pantomime would be to more sophisticated children.

'The family had some mild dissipation this week; the Episcopal Band of Hope gave an entertainment and acted a little play. I took the four to see it;

it was Flora's first entertainment of any kind, and she was greatly excited. It was very pretty, with fairies and a Santa Claus. Isobel loved it. "Oh, I would just give my eyes to be one of these fairies!" she cried. I wonder what she would say to *Peter Pan* if I could take her.

'Another excitement was last night when I took them to the Club. It does not take much to raise them to the seventh heaven. To have supper with Daddy and Mama and to get an egg with it and sit up late is quite enough even without the entertainment. Ronald and Sheriff Boswell were on last night's committee as entertainers; they both go conscientiously, but it would be difficult to say which looks most unhappy when there. They wander about like lost souls, not knowing what to do, till at last the happy idea strikes them of entertaining each other, and they go off into a corner with a draught-board and take no further part'.

At the beginning of March with Flora's birthday just over and Peter's coming in a week three of us were at last given regular pocket-money. I was ten years old and Allan seven. Mother describes our problems. 'They had great difficulty in scraping together sixpence for the book they gave to Flora, as the Christmas presents had cleared their banks. So I have promised the three older children a Saturday penny which they can claim as their due. Alasdair earned a few pennies by crocheting squares, but in a generous mood he took a collecting-card at the Sunday School, so off his pennies went to feed a famine orphan at the rate of three pence ha' penny a day. They are all feeling like millionaires today with 2d apiece, but Peter's birthday this week will probably clear away half of it. Such are the ups and downs of finance'.

Meanwhile Alasdair had joined me in Miss Baxter's room after spending only six months with Miss Mackie — a remarkable rate of progress. Miss Baxter was the daughter of Captain Baxter, the 'genial skipper' of the *Glencoe*: she was quite young, in fact she left us at the end of this school-year to be married, and I was chosen to make a speech and to present her with a silver-backed brush and comb for a wedding-present from the class. I wore my best white dress of well-starched Swiss embroidery to grace the occasion, and the scene of farewell was so moving that Miss Baxter shed tears. I wept and embraced her; only the boys remained dry-eyed. On thinking it over we were rather puzzled by this wave of feeling, since Miss Baxter, though lively and interesting, had been a fierce teacher: we had trembled at her cutting tongue, and many a little aching paw had been nursed under the desks when she had vented her exasperation round the class with a ruler. Probably the rages and the tears were both signs of a nervous temperament, stirred to wrath by the dumb stupidity and inattention of a too-large class in a stuffy room on a pouring wet afternoon, but touched by our little contributions and shy well-wishing.

Indeed it was not surprising that she should feel the strain. In the junior division of Portree school the children were not streamed or moved up yearly; they advanced from one class to another when their teacher thought they were ready. Miss Baxter's room was the terminus of this process; it contained the Qualifying class where the brighter pupils were prepared for the examination that would pass them into the secondary division of the school; their ages varied from eight (Alasdair's age) to eleven or twelve according to their rate of progress through the previous standards. But as well as these hopeful aspirants she had to teach the Supplementary class which contained the slowest children in the school who had crawled their way up, and were marking time till their fourteenth birthday set them free. Poor Miss Baxter had to switch from inspiring children who might eventually go to university, to giving some kind of occupation to the awkward squad in the side-desks, great boys who would start a fight if she took her eyes off them for long. She had to hold up the lamp of knowledge with one hand and crack a lion-tamer's whip with the other; no wonder if she sometimes confused her categories. One result of this almost impossible arrangement was that each class was left to work by itself a good deal while Miss Baxter dealt with the other. I could finish my set stint quickly, and pass the time in writing a poem, or in reading and re-reading from our poetry-book, the third part of J. C. Smith's *Book of Verse for Boys and Girls*, still one of the best of all school anthologies. I discovered Gray's *Elegy in a Country Churchyard*, and Milton's *L'Allegro* and *Il Penseroso*, also his *Ode on the Morning of Christ's Nativity* which I used to read aloud to myself in a recess by the seashore where I had fixed a cross of pine branches among the rocks.

Alasdair worked with me till the end of the school year in June when I moved on and left him. At first I was pleased to have him there, but a week later mother writes:- 'Poor Isobel is finding that it is a mixed blessing to have Alasdair in the same class. Generally she can beat him easily, but occasionally he beats her in spelling, and then it is not quite so nice as you might think. To play second fiddle well was never one of Isobel's accomplishments. They are now learning what they call "Laws of Health," which is rather like our first aid course. It amuses me to hear them grinding away at the frontal, temporal, parietal and occipital bones of the head, and the nitrogenous element in food. If it would induce them to eat fat and take what is set before them it would be most welcome instruction, but will it? — nay verily!'

Allan was also doing well at school, though when he began to learn history he brought home some unusual pieces of information — 'The revelation was going on in Scotland while Queen Victoria was spending her happy years in France.' He was not as virtuous as he had been during his early days, and mother was surprised to hear that an Inspector had thought him one of the best in his class, as he was often too fond of fun and mischief to attend properly, and one day was whipped four times for laughing and inattention. At home his inquiring mind was nearly the end of him. 'He gave us all a fright by holding his celluloid collar over the lamp to see what would happen. What did happen surprised him. Celluloid, I believe, is just gun-cotton, so it went up in a fine blaze. He threw it on the floor, and had Maggie not been there it would have set fire to the bed-draperies. He still bears the mark of a small burn on his cheek to remind him not to try experiments with celluloid collars'.

At the end of March, when the memory of his former suffering was still fresh, poor Alasdair had to be taken again to the dentist's improvised surgery. This time his cheerful courage failed him, and no wonder! 'Poor boy, he has had a bad time of it, first with toothache and then with the dentist. I found two of his big permanent teeth badly decayed and took him to the dentist who happened to be visiting Portree. Alas and alack! Alasdair was not a credit to his family, and the interviews were painful to all concerned. Probably the previous toothache had knocked his nerves to bits, but he behaved very badly. The dentist put in something to kill the nerves and I must say they died hard. For hours he was in agony. I took him for his first visit, but I had enough of it, so made Ronald take him for the second. Tomorrow it is my turn again, when I hope things will be finished and we shall have peace'. A series of visits to a dentist who seems to have been sparing or inefficient with his pain-killers would be an ordeal to anyone, let alone to a child of eight.

From April to June of that year Alasdair, Allan and I spent most weekday evenings and Saturdays at our fort. It was in a turn of the path that went round the Lump, quite near our home, a wide jutting ledge of rock among the cliffs, shadowed by an ash-tree. We built turf walls all round and laid in various kinds of ammunition; we could either climb up from below or drop from the crag above, which raised interesting problems of attack and defence when we divided against each other, though most of the time we played as a united company of outlaws holding our fort against all comers. Flora and Peter were too small for the game but we three were near enough in age to make happy playmates — 'they don't seem to regard Allan as inferior at all,' said mother. I should think not indeed! He was the most lovable of the family, always well, never moody or quarrelsome, very inventive and eager, with an inexhaustible spirit of enjoyment. We shared our adventures with two other little boys from Miss Baxter's room at school: Ian Morrison, a friendly intelligent child with honey-coloured hair and grey eyes, and Joseph Fleming who was dark and gay and sweet-natured. He had a beautiful singing voice and was quite unselfconscious about it; one afternoon when Miss Baxter asked if someone would give us a song he stood up smiling and filled the room with his silver treble, pleased to give pleasure, but without a trace of conceit, while we all sat enchanted. That I was the only girl in that company of little boys did not seem of much significance to any of us: difference of sex was no more important at that time than having dark or fair hair, though Joseph and I carried on a kind of innocent courtship; we liked taking hands and doing things together and having long talks and occasionally kissing each other. What did surprise me was that one morning when Ian and I were alone together at the fort he declared that he loved me and was jealous of Joseph, so to make him feel happier I kissed him too — after all, I quite often kissed my brothers — but I really liked Joseph best. He was the first Catholic I had met except Father John Macmillan long ago, and mother describes a service that would have delighted present-day unifiers.

'Yesterday the children spent most of the day at their fort. They had out their kite which went well, and they flew the flag you sent them. They had a service taken by their chaplain Joseph Fleming. "You see," as Isobel explained, "he is the most sacred of us all even if he is a Catholic, for he serves before the altar, but he has promised to write a Protestant sermon for us." She brought home his sermon to read to me, and it was quite edifying. Before and after it he had repeated Catholic prayers, and they had sung, "I think when I read that sweet story of old," so there was nothing bigoted in their service'.

The summer of 1914 was even more golden and joyful than that of the previous year. At the end of June mother writes: 'The children are all in the best of health and spirits, with bare legs and canvas shoes, and summer frocks and suits which are ready for the tub nearly every night. I tell Maggie that if she has more washing she has less darning, but the last washing was a caution!' No one except father had any fears about the future: I have heard that during this year he said to a friend that he was sure Germany was a danger to Europe, and then, looking out from the library window to the bay and Ben Tianavaig he added, 'If it comes to war I know what I shall be fighting for'. But for us the summer was pure delight.

'No sense had we of ills to come,
  Nor care beyond today.'

In mid-July we had a glorious day at sea in a yacht which belonged to the proprietor of Raasay, the guest whose coffee Peter had nearly ruined by shaking knife-powder into the grinder. He was not in Skye himself at the time, but he evidently wanted to keep his crew employed and to return father's hospitality: it was an ideal state of affairs both for us and for our parents. We had the run of a large interesting steam-yacht all day without having to mind our manners in the presence of a strange grown-up, and they had no nervous fears that we might inadvertently do or say something that had to be blushed for. Raasay House where Boswell and Johnson spent such a merry time has an amazing view: it looks across the Sound to the great cone of Glamaig rising from sea-level above Loch Sligachan with the dark line of the Black Cuillins against the westering sun.

'We had a lovely day on Tuesday on board Mr. McCosh's yacht the *Aerolite*. When I wakened the rain was coming down in buckets, and five very sad little children appeared at breakfast. But when the yacht steamed into the bay about ten things looked more cheerful. Uncle Norman, Catriona, Ronald and I and the five children formed the party, and there were no hosts to be polite to, so we felt perfectly at home, as if the yacht belonged to us. There were endless places for the children to explore; upper decks, lower decks, cabins, bedrooms and dining-room, ladders to climb up and steps to run down, engines to watch, and mysterious cooking operations. They had not a dull moment. Soon the day brightened up; the sun came out in a blue sky and the clouds disappeared. We sailed north to Staffin; soon our nostrils were tickled by pleasant aromas of roasting mutton and cauliflower, and we were invited to a delightful repast followed by coffee.

'When we came on deck again we were going round the end of Rona to the back of Raasay. It was all new to me, and it was lovely to sit on the deck and glide along the blue water. By and by Peter got sleepy and we tucked him up in the cabin for an hour or two. The other children played at hide-and-seek all over the ship, and made friends with the sailors and with the steward who gave them biscuits and the captain who let them see through his field-glasses. Then there was an aroma of hot toast, and again we went downstairs to a delicious tea. When we finished we had reached Raasay bay and were rowed ashore to visit the house. No one was staying there, so we were shown through it and admired the wonderful views from the windows. We saw the room where Dr. Johnson slept and the bed he slept in. Then we had to hurry on board again because Uncle Norman wanted to catch the mail. We told the boys that they were invited to Glenhinisdale with Uncle Norman; there was jumping for joy and a hurried gathering of gear, and off they went, very happy and excited. I have not heard from them yet, but I am sure they are having a good time at the Glen in this fine weather'.

But then, all too soon after that joyful day, on August 2nd it comes. 'Isn't it dreadful news about the war! Ronald is very much excited about it. He is expecting a telegram requiring his services, and then he will have to go off. It is too dreadful to think about; I cannot realise it at all. He might not come home again for months'.

And so the war shattered that island summer of long sunshine and tranquility. Father was a captain in the Territorial Fourth Battalion of the Queen's Own Cameron Highlanders: by annual camps and frequent drill-parades he had been training for years to serve his country in a war which his historical sense and his knowledge of European politics had warned him was inevitable, though nothing could have told him of its length and horror, or that within a year he would have been wounded in the confused useless battle of Festubert, and within another year dead after long suffering in hospital. Under his command he had the flower of the island: young men from distant crofts who had attended Portree School, and men like himself whose age might have exempted them (he was forty-eight) but who would never have made any such demand. On a morning of soft rain they marched down to the pier with a swing of the kilt and a skirl of the pipes; then as the *Gael* moved out into the bay the men on board and the sorrowful crowd on land sang 'God Save the King.'

I was not in Portree when war broke out as I had been taken south by mother's cousin Liza Bertram who had been visiting us, to have my eyes re-tested. On the boat we made the acquaintance of two delightful American ladies, Miss Amey Aldrich and Miss Hope Smith who were sitting near us and were amused to hear me entertaining Cousin Liza by reciting Macaulay's *Armada* with dramatic fervour. They joined us for the journey from Mallaig to Glasgow, and when I met Miss Aldrich many years later in New York she said that she had been very surprised to hear a Hebridean child of ten quoting Lowell to them. I do not remember this, but father used to chant passages of the *Biglow Papers* to himself, and sometimes read them to me, as he used to read me Kipling's *Barrack-room Ballads*, so perhaps what I quoted was the too appropriate verse:

'I do believe whatever trash
   'll keep the people in blindness:-
That we the Mexican can thrash
   Right into brotherly kindness;
That bombshells, grape, and powder 'n ball
   Air goodwill's strongest magnets;
That peace, to make it stick at all,
   Must be druv in with bagnets.'

He especially liked the last two lines, so I was probably quoting father rather than Lowell.

Aunt Agnes brought me back in September. For some absurd reason connected with war-time security all passengers boarding the Skye boat at Mallaig had to give their names, addresses and ages to be laboriously written down by the purser before they were allowed to set foot on the deck. I was all ears as my unfortunate aunt paused on the last question and looked at me desperately, obviously wondering whether she dared refuse to answer, but she was a good citizen and a truthful woman, so at last she murmured 'Forty.' To my joy this gave a key-figure from which with a few innocent questions — 'How much older are you than Aunt Agnes?' — we could find out our parents' ages, which in these days were kept from children as closely as the facts of birth.

The next few letters tell how father and his men are training in Bedford, and describe the disturbed ant-hill activity of ambulance-lectures and sewing-parties that marks the beginning of a war on the home-front. Flora, then six years old, had another tonsil-operation, this time performed with two doctors, chloroform and a nurse; the previous cruel snatch had been as ineffective as it was agonising. She had hardly recovered from this when she had a very severe and dangerous illness; it was probably appendicitis which developed into peritonitis, as at that period on that distant island it would have been impossible to take the child to a surgeon in time. Aunt Agnes stayed for nearly two months to help mother with the nursing, and together they pulled her through. The only thing that comforted the poor little creature in her suffering was to have *The Ugly Duckling* read aloud to her; no other story would do, and mother and Aunt Agnes knew it almost by heart before she recovered. Probably she was soothed by the joy and beauty of the ending after all the wretchedness that the duckling endures.

Father at Bedford was so anxious about Flora and so distressed at being far away during her danger that his health suffered, but early in November he came home on leave, to everyone's delight. Mother describes her precarious happiness.

'We have been so happy this week. The weather was good and Ronald was well and bright. We have been out a lot together, walking or visiting, and we have had our friends the Macleans and Boswells to tea. The children meanwhile were chased downstairs; they did not like it, but they can have some attention later, and I wanted Ronald to have a good time. But on Thursday night a letter came from his Adjutant saying that the Ross-shires were off to the front, and that he had been privately informed that the Camerons were to go next, so Ronald was to hold himself in instant readiness to be recalled. It gave me a dreadful shock; I felt as if the telegraph boy was already on his way to summon him. Now that a few days have passed we are lulled into security again, and are hoping he will have his full time till Friday morning. One would be glad not to be able to think or feel these days'.

Meanwhile we were getting on as best we could downstairs in the nurseries. Aunt Agnes read aloud very well, and had been entertaining us during her long visit with some of Kipling's humorous stories — *My Lord the Elephant*, and *Brugglesmith*. As we thought drunk men were irresistibly comic objects we enjoyed them very much.

'Peter fell into the bath with all his clothes on; they had been shooed downstairs and he thought it a fit occasion to sail his boats. Another night Allan was making toast and burned his hand, but these are minor incidents. They are missing their Aunt Agnes, though I try to take her place at reading-time after lessons. Alasdair and Isobel have got *Brugglesmith* by heart, and give it in dialogue at odd moments, so she has a lot to answer for'.

Father was not recalled, but mother felt very desolate after their last embrace in the house — he hated public farewells — and comforted herself with hopes and rumours. 'I had a very sore heart on parting with Ronald. I managed to keep bright and to give him a cheery send-off, but when I saw him disappear into the cold dark morning I felt as if my heart would break. But since then one or two things have cheered me a little. Ronald was convinced that they were to be off to the front in a day or two, but yesterday I heard that one of his sergeants was coming home on leave, which shows they are not leaving Bedford so soon as they expected. I also heard that they were getting thinner tunics and helmets, which looks as if they might be going to Egypt or India'.

That autumn a severe epidemic of scarlet fever broke out in Portree, and the school was closed for four weeks. Patients were taken to the little fever-hospital in a sinister horse-drawn ambulance with a large hood which looked like a covered wagon from a Western film. Many of the boys and girls in the secondary department of the school came from distant parts of Skye or from North Uist and lodged in the village; they had met with so little infection in these remote places that they were especially susceptible. Early in 1915 there was another severe epidemic, this time of measles, from which

Peter, Allan, Isobel, Alasdair and Flora in November 1914.

we all suffered; it also broke out among the Highland regiments training in Bedford, and twenty-eight young soldiers in the Camerons died of it.

Mother describes our pastimes at the beginning of this long holiday. 'Alasdair has a tickling cough so I have kept him in bed for the last day or so; he has been quite happy reading, crocheting and enjoying his meals. The other children have been out a good deal as the weather has been bright and dry. Allan and Flora have been playing with the bicycle. Neither of them can ride it, yet they have some funny way of their own of sticking on, Flora in front and Allan behind, and come rushing down the brae in front of the house in fine style. Flora is getting fat and rosy again; you would never think she had been so ill.

'Isobel has been taking long walks with one of the little Macrae girls, and comes home happy and hungry. Last night I was quite anxious about her; when tea-time came it was dark and she had not come home. Then I remembered that she had said something about climbing Fingal's Seat. She turned up before very long, tired and rosy. Nanette's watch had stopped, which had upset their calculations, and the dark had come on quickly. They were rather frightened, but they did get well up Fingal's Seat, and had enjoyed their walk immensely'.

The Camerons continued to train in Bedford. 'Ronald's latest news is that they do not expect to be sent to France immediately. Some of them are disappointed, but I am very pleased that they should enjoy the comforts of their native land for a time longer. Ronald has been writing cheerfully since he went back; he feels that his men are much more able to give a good account of themselves, and events abroad have gone better than he expected. He says he has a strong conviction that he will come back safe and sound. That means a great deal from Ronald who is constitutionally not inclined to take too rosy a view of the future. His letters have cheered me wonderfully'.

She goes on to describe a typical War Office muddle; some young soldiers on leave recalled when in sight of the island. It seems that in these days they had to pay their own fares, which would be considerable from Bedford to Skye.

'Has he told you about the poor Skye boys who came all the way from Bedford, a cold journey of a day and a night, and when they reached Kyle and were almost in sight of their homes, were turned back again and had to face the long cold journey back without food or any comforts except what they could get at the station. I was visiting some of their friends here, and they were *bitterly* disappointed. And after all there seemed no reason for their peremptory recall from the War Office. Ronald hopes they will pay the fares for them, but that is doubtful, so they will be left badly out of pocket as well. He says that, soldiers though they were, they nearly cried when they saw the *Glencoe* going away without them'.

Peter's father came to see his little son. 'I had a visit from Peter's father one market day last week. As I was busy I asked him if he would like to take Peter for a walk. He was delighted with the idea, so I put on Peter's nice new brown coat and hat, and he and Alasdair and his father went off together. He evidently took him round and introduced him to all his friends, for the two boys came home with two sixpences, a shilling, a penny, a bag of chocolates and a bag of apples, and Allan thought he had missed a good thing'.

With winter and wartime, transport was becoming more and more difficult, but Eigg was always an awkward island to reach. 'We had a visitor this afternoon, the late Mr. Thomson's factor. He left his home on the mainland last Wednesday to go to Eigg, but it was too stormy to land there, or at Mallaig, or at Kyle, so he was carried on to Portree where he will have to kick his heels for three days, and perhaps get to Eigg next Wednesday, unless he is carried past again'.

Then there is another domestic disaster; water was always the enemy in Skye. 'A week ago I noticed a leak in the green room ceiling, and went myself to the mason to ask him to come and see to it. Needless to say, he did not come. Next day the drip had grown worse, so I went again and left word for him to call and see to it. Again he did not come. By the evening it was beginning to go through the floor into Mr. Fraser's office, so I again sent word, but it was too late to do anything. That night the windows of heaven opened, and when I went in next morning all my baths and basins were overflowing, part of the ceiling was down, the carpet full of lime and sandy water, and the office below was also flooded. I got the mason *then*, but he said it would be suicide for him to go up a ladder and examine the roof, so I had to watch helplessly till he judged it safe to go up and mend it. My carpet looks as if it would never be decent again'.

A week later, on Sunday December 6th, our long holiday is nearly at an end, and we have been making good use of the spare-room upheaval. 'I am glad to inform you that school re-opens on Tuesday, so you can picture me joyfully turning my little brood out of doors. They have had nearly four weeks' holiday, and it has rained and poured and blown great guns nearly all the time, so they have scarcely got out of doors at all, and their high spirits indoors have nearly equalled the great gales outside. For a day or two I had my green room carpet propped up on chairs and a fire lit to dry it. That made a wigwam for them, so they got all sorts of weird garments and transferred the contents of their paintboxes to their faces and played Red Indians — *five* Red Indians, and a little girl who came in to play with them made six. Six Red Indians! — you can imagine the noise, and the state of the bathroom towels when the paint was finally transferred from their faces. They nearly made themselves sick by smoking peace-pipes without much result as far as peace was concerned. At last the carpet is dried and down again, and it looks not too bad, though it was very difficult to stretch and lay. The hole in the ceiling will have to wait till spring'.

Lady Macdonald and her daughter, the Honourable Miss Iona, stayed in Portree during the winter months. Miss Iona invited the boy scouts up to the Lodge while the school was closed to learn patriotic songs; Alasdair who had a sweet voice and was a member of the boys' Gaelic choir went every morning, to mother's relief — 'it gives him something to do, wet or dry'. Lady Macdonald organised sewing-parties for the Red Cross, which produced a good deal of smothered annoyance.

'We meet at three, sew until quarter to five and then have tea. We make the garments of a soft grey flannelette, and Lady Macdonald insists that they be *entirely hand-sewn!* It makes us all very cross to sit laboriously stitching up long seams that would be so much quicker and better done by machine. The limit is reached when we have to *stitch by hand* round collars and cuffs and down the front. We have all forgotten how to do that sort of thing neatly, besides we feel that the poor Tommies, after a week or two in the trenches, are not likely to insist on having their garments hand-sewn, but her Ladyship is quite firm about it, so we keep our feelings to ourselves till we get out, and then we think how much there is to do, how little we have done, and how much we *could* have done if only we had our machines'.

Of course an aristocrat of Lady Macdonald's generation would never have worn an undergarment that was not exquisitely hand-sewn, and none but the best was good enough for our gallant defenders. But it must have been exasperating for mother who could never have kept five children clothed and a credit to her without her trusty sewing-machine. A week later she writes: 'I was at Lady Macdonald's Red Cross sewing-meeting yesterday. It is nightshirts we are making, and I have been two days over a pair of sleeves, and I am still stitching round the cuffs. I was rather far from the lamp, so could not see very well, which did not improve matters. We hope that the poor Tommies who receive them are not delirious or too active in bed, or they may put their shoulders out at the yokes or sleeves, to judge by some of the sewing'.

It is an interesting point that no one dared to argue or rebel: to have suggested anything as non-U as making the garments by sewing-machine was out of the question. They all sat round, painfully stitching by the light of an oil-lamp, and only expressed their rueful feelings to each other on the way home. It was a fairly long walk from the village to the Lodge, and the journey back in total darkness, through the woods, across the Scorrybreck bridge and by the shore, must have been very difficult; I do not think electric torches were much in use at that time. The patriotic ladies who attended the sewing-parties were making a considerable effort to get there, which could so easily have produced more of the large strong masculine nightshirts required by the Red Cross.

1915: Before And After Festubert

In 1914 we had to go to school on Christmas Day, and had only one day's holiday, to make up for the long closure of the school during the epidemic. This was on New Year's Day, at that time more generally celebrated in Scotland than Christmas, that Popish-sounding feast which the stricter Presbyterians thought it positively wrong to observe. As usual there was a shortage of milk during the winter, but nevertheless we had a festive time.

'We have had a happy New Year's Day, the one and only holiday the children had. We had a present of a handsome turkey from Ronald's brother in Barra, so it was an easy matter to provide a sumptuous dinner. Catriona spent the whole day with us, coming for breakfast at half-past eight. Mr. Morrison gave us a very nice little New Year service, partly in English and partly in Gaelic, when I could apply my mind to solving the providing of a New Year dinner and tea for ten people with one penny worth of milk. However at the last moment I managed to get some more, so the bread sauce and other extras were forthcoming. We had a fine gramophone concert and lots of games with the children, and a very happy evening'.

Early in the year mother made some changes in her household, as a war-time economy, and because her children were old enough to do without a full-time nurse, since Flora was nearly seven and Peter nearly five. Nana left us, and Maggie took her place as housemaid, though she also kept an eye on the younger children and supervised a girl in her teens called Flora MacIntosh who had been engaged to look after them. But soon the house was stricken with pestilence, with scarlet fever in the kitchen and measles in the nursery. The first alarm was about Mary the cook.

'Word came up about the middle of the day that Mary was feeling ill and would I come down to see her. I found her looking very poorly with sore throat and head and high temperature, and sick and miserable. I at once thought she had scarlet fever, and she was convinced of it herself. My heart sank; the last person in the house that you want to take scarlet fever is your cook-general. I got her off to bed and sent for the doctor. He did not turn up till nearly ten at night, and then said he could not tell till next day, but he would come first thing in the morning, which turned out to be nearly two o'clock in the afternoon. However by this time she seemed much better and no rash had appeared, so I was not so anxious. He said then that it was not scarlet fever, just a bad chill or influenza or something of that sort. He promised to come tonight to paint her throat which is still very sore, but it is nearly ten and he has not turned up, so I don't expect he will come now. She is still rather miserable, but we are all relieved that it is not to be a six weeks business'.

It was evidently difficult to distinguish scarlet fever from the many kinds of sore throats available, but during the next week Flora the nursemaid fell ill with such unmistakeable symptoms that she was packed off to hospital on the Wednesday. This put us all into quarantine for ten days, and brought back doubts about Mary. She seemed well on the way to recovery, but her illness might after all be a mild case of scarlet fever caught from the same source as Flora's. She was kept in seclusion for some days, but by Sunday it looked as if she had quite regained her usual health.

'The problem was, what to do with Mary. The village folk are scared about the spread of the fever, so that I knew that whatever I did would be fully known and freely criticised. She seemed all right, and did not at all like the idea of being kept in lonely confinement in a fever-stricken room in the garret; however we thought it best to leave her there for a few days to see if she began to peel. As there was no sign today of her having had, or being about to have, fever Dr. Fletcher allowed me to let her have her carbolic bath and come downstairs. He is coming tomorrow to disinfect the rooms, but if I see any further developments I must isolate her again'.

And on the very next day it looked as if they had all been wrong. 'We were rejoicing at having Mary downstairs again, especially today with a big washing on hand. You can imagine my feelings when Maggie came up to tell me that she thought Mary's hands were beginning to peel. I went at once for Dr. Fletcher who is Medical Officer; he said he couldn't be certain, but she had better go up to the hospital for a day or two to be under observation. So poor Mary had to go off weeping in the big ambulance-van with a small crowd of interested spectators taking it all in. I doubt if we shall see her again inside six weeks'.

It was hard work to run a large house with only one maid instead of three, and without the mechanical aids that are taken for granted nowadays. We did not even have our trusty gardener Willie Ross, for he had gone to the war, and his successor who was better at lifting the bottle than the spade gave nothing but trouble during the next few months. Everyone had to lend a hand.

'Alasdair cleans the boots, carries in coals and chops wood; Allan cleans knives and runs messages, and Isobel is really useful. She makes the beds with me and looks after the two smaller ones. Yesterday she was fearfully proud of herself when she scrubbed out the nursery floor. We have managed wonderfully, but when you think of ten lamps and four fires every day to keep going, and all the boots and dishes and rooms that have to be done you can understand that we had our hands full. We hadn't even Harrison the gardener to help us, for he hadn't *quite* got over his New Year and was spending the first week of it in bed. However Maggie rose to the occasion and did her best, though she was often tired enough.

'Ronald is having a hard week of it too. His two lieutenants are ill, one of them seriously. The weather was bad and the measles still spreading. Two more of his men have died, and he had the painful duty of superintending their funerals and writing to their parents as well as his other work'.

But a week later Mary was restored to us as good as new. 'I think my news this week will surprise you; Mary has just come home again. She arived an hour ago looking better than I have seen her for a long time; her week's rest in hospital seems to have agreed with her. Dr. Fletcher called to say he was convinced she had not had scarlet fever; it was only her hands that peeled, and he thought that might happen after an illness with a temperature when she put her hands into hot water after a week in bed. We are very glad to have her back for this house cannot be worked with one maid, however willing. All the same there have been compensations. I have been frightfully busy, but I have enjoyed the simpler style of living. I have enjoyed having the freedom of the sink, and going into the kitchen to make potato scones after dinner. I have enjoyed the scrubbing and cleaning, and the feeling of satisfaction when every corner was straight, and the house looking tidier than usual. And — tell it not in Gath — I have enjoyed being shut off from the rest of the community for the time being. I have not spoken to a soul outside the house except Dr. Fletcher for a week, and it has been a great rest'.

Since the whole family was in quarantine we had all been available to help during this difficult time, but on January 18th our education was resumed. At eleven years old I was becoming less poetic and more practical: any parents who are beginning to despair of small stubborn tantrum-ridden girls may be comforted to learn that they will probably become friendly and useful beings as time passes and they learn sense. 'I am sending the children back to school tomorrow, but Dr. Fletcher expects it will be closed very soon. It is sad to see how their education has been interrupted this year. Isobel has been a great help to me; she is a very business-like little person when she pleases. She has taken complete charge of the two nurseries and does them out every day. She puts the two little ones to bed and gives them bath and supper. I wish you could see her with her drugget apron and sleeves tucked up and wee pigtail, looking so important'.

Sure enough, by January 31st the school was closed again, and we did not go back till the end of March. Mother describes some of our employments. 'I have had the wee ones out every afternoon in this fine weather; sometimes the two boys joined us, but more often they preferred adventures of their own over the heights above the Black Rock. It is a blessing that they are so nearly of an age. They are good companions, and it makes them independent of the village boys who are sometimes rough.

'I have enjoyed my rambles with my two youngest, and this conversation may amuse you. They were speaking about the smith. Flora remarked that she had never seen him, though she knew the joiner. Whereupon Peter: — "Oh Flora, I saw the smith, and he's a *big black man!*" — then, after a pause

— "I think he's the man who puts the bad people into the fire when they're dead." Mr. Ferguson the smith who, decent man, leads a large family into the Auld Kirk every Sunday would not be flattered if he heard him!'

We even went out for an evening's pleasure, though conditions left something to be desired. 'I took the three older children to a magic lantern lecture by Mr. Morrison about our mission to India. It was an icy cold night and there was not a spark of fire in the church, and the lantern smoked, and we had to wait outside till the doors were opened though we arrived only three minutes before the time. In the middle of the lecture the lantern went out and there was an interval to set it going again, and the children were restless, and thought every black face was meant for a joke and every idol for a huge joke — so it was not quite so nice as you might think. But as it was the only evening entertainment the children have been out to this winter they were not too critical. The mere fact of sitting up late outweighed the discomfort of frozen feet'.

Early in February father came home on leave again, to see his island and his children for the last time. The milk supply from the Home Farm had been stopped because one of their maids had developed scarlet fever; this raised problems for a family brought up on porridge. Condensed milk in these days was a sticky yellowish substance with a peculiar sweet taste of its own.

'To complicate matters our milk supply has been stopped for a month! So how to bring up children without either milk or education is the question. I have the promise of some milk when a certain cow sees fit to calve, but it does not seem in any hurry to enjoy the pleasures of maternity. Meanwhile we do not so badly on condensed milk, and are even using it for porridge. Some of the children like it, some don't, but all take it. Maids don't like, but I have argued them into trying. Ronald also does not like it, and I have failed to make him try, so you see that my powers of persuasion have their limits'.

But a few days later I was inconsiderate enough to develop an attack of measles so severe that I needed nursing night and day. The virulent form of the illness that had broken out in Bedford had been carried back to Skye by soldiers on leave, and spread through the island. Poor mother writes: 'It was very hard to have Isobel so ill during Ronald's short visit. I only had one walk with him, and I had been looking forward to seeing friends and having good times together. However one must take what comes'.

Father set out for Bedford on a Thursday, but his regiment had left for Southampton and France at 3 a.m. on the Friday night while he was still travelling from Skye. Surprisingly he was not sent on to join them, but kept for another month on training duties in Bedford. He missed his men and his friends and felt out of things, but mother was thankful to know that he would have a roof over his head and a bed to lie in when she heard the winter storms of hail and sleet battering on the windows.

After five days of misery my measles began to improve and I made a rapid recovery, but soon the others were stricken, and mother was especially anxious about Flora who had been so dangerously ill last October. She writes to her sister Mary who was a nurse: 'Flora is the one who gives me most concern. I had a fright the other morning. She had a temperature of 102 at night, and I thought she looked very tired in the morning. I took her temperature and found it only 95.4; her hands and feet were quite cool. I gave her a stimulant and a hot-water-bottle, but when I took it again it was still only 95.6. The rash is not out yet, but Dr. Macdonald thinks it will be out tomorrow. She is such a tender wee creature that I shall be very thankful when she begins to mend'.

A week later she writes to thank Aunt Mary for toys and books: her patients are improving, but she is still anxious about her exhausted little Flora. 'The doctor was here today and thinks she will be all right, but she will need care and nursing. She is very limp still, not wanting at all to sit up or move about in bed. Her heart is missing beats as it did when she was ill before, but the doctor thinks it will come right in time. I am to give her a stimulant every five hours and keep her very quiet'.

The young doctor who had come to Portree in 1910 was so erratic in his attendance and so uncertain in his diagnosis that when anyone was seriously ill mother sent for Dr. Macdonald of Uig who was the most skilful medical man on the island. But the distance from Portree led to difficulties in these days when there were no telephones on Skye. The letter to Aunt Mary continues: 'You are well off to have the doctor at the end of a telephone instead of fifteen miles away. You feel so helpless when any difficulty arises. I got Dr. Macdonald's account the other day for last year: it came to £18. It is a lot of money, but it includes both Flora's illness and the operation on her throat, and when one thinks that humanly speaking we owe her life to him, one cannot grudge it. He is getting a motor car which will make things easier. Uig is such an ungetatable place for letters; you have to write early in the day, and then you don't get an answer the next day but the day after, so it is no use to write for advice. You must telegraph, but it is not easy to give details in a telegram'.

Indeed the mind boggles at the thought of a consultation by telegram, with intimate medical details being scanned by postal clerks, and the chance of mistakes in transmission.

Alasdair and Allam were rapidly returning to normal, and mother vividly describes the difference between little boys ill and little boys recovering. 'Last week they were so good and quiet and kept their beds so tidy and were so grateful for all you did for them that it was a pleasure to nurse them, but this week it is a different story. They want to fling things at each other, and to tease Peter who is at the irritable stage. The beds are never straight for two minutes. When I opened the door one time I found them in a scrimmage on the floor; they scuttled back to bed and then explained that a penny had rolled out of Alasdair's hand and the temptation to grab it first had been too strong for human nature. Last week I brought them nice little mugs of soup or milk; now there is no satisfying them. When I ask them what they will have the answer is, "Everything that I can get!" So you can see that they are well on the road to recovery'.

Early in March Alasdair and Allan are up and about again. 'They are both losing the pretty pink and white complexions they had when they first got up, and their hands and knees are rapidly coming back to what they consider their natural colour — a healthy grey'. Even Flora is improving. 'She can sit up in bed and paint now. Dr. Macdonald says there is nothing really wrong except that the muscles of her heart are a little weak, but that will pass away as she grows stronger. She is to get up for a little while early this week, but he advises me to take special care of her for a fortnight'. But Peter who was the last to fall ill had been afflicted by a malady more agonising than measles. 'The poor little boy's recovery is being complicated by severe attacks of toothache. I don't know what to do for him. I would rather have a whole family ill with measles than one with bad toothache. He can't eat properly and has got quite thin'. She goes on to tell how she wrapped Flora and Peter in quilts and carried them in to the pink room bed, so that the two convalescents could celebrate their birthdays, which came so close together, with the rest of the family. 'Everything went merry as a marriage bell, till in the middle of the tea what Peter calls his "teethack" began, so it was not quite so nice as you might think!'

Fortunately the dentist was due in Portree next week, and Peter was taken to his improvised surgery. The account of his treatment makes one shudder; the child was only just five years old, and hardly recovered from a severe attack of measles. The stoicism with which he bore it was very characteristic.

'We had a time of it last week with Peter and his "teethack"! We could not get the dentist till Wednesday forenoon, and it was only a lucky chance that he happened to be in Portree at all; he won't be back till June. He found the teeth pretty bad, and stopped four and pulled one. You know how Peter sits when he is shy — as if he were mesmerised. He was like that; he never moved except to open and shut his mouth when told. He was over an hour in the dentist's hands, and he was just out of bed, so it must have been an ordeal. He did not make any fuss even when he had the big one out, which was the last thing; it was taken out without cocaine or anything else, so it was a big tug. There was an abscess at the root, and the dentist thought he would have less trouble afterwards if he did not deaden it. Peter's feelings found vent later in the remark, "Mama, I wish the Germans would get their teeth pulled out."'

By March 21st we were all back at school except Flora — 'she is bright and lively, but looks pale and big-eyed yet'. Her education had been very much interrupted; she had begun school happily in April 1914, but her severe illnesses made regular attendance impossible till April 1915 when she was seven years old. But she was a steady calm little thing and made good progress once she had started. Peter began to go to school at the same time.

Meanwhile father was still in Bedford. 'He is in command of two hundred men and eight officers, also in charge of thirty horses. He has to attend the orderly room, see after correspondence, draw up schemes for the training of the men week by week, punish misdemeanours and so on. It is more responsible and more interesting work than he had before. He also has to go out with them for route marches and night entrenchments, so he is kept busy'. The Camerons had been in the front trenches soon after their arrival in France, but there had been a lull in the fighting. 'There have been no casualties so far, but one of the officers had a German bullet through his glengarry bonnet. I am thankful that it was not Ronald's head that was under that glengarry!'

Two weeks later the news is more serious. 'They have been in the thick of the severe fighting at Neuve Chapelle. Many of their officers have been wounded or killed; the officer who took charge of Ronald's men is among the wounded. This week has been a time of great anxiety in Portree; we are like one big family up here, more so than ever since the war began. We all know when anyone gets a letter from the front; indeed the postman will tell us at the door that letters came today from Donald or Murdo or Angus, and by next day we know what Donald or Murdo or Angus had to say. This week day after day no letter arrived for anyone. We knew that they were in the big fight, and then we knew that some of the officers had been hit, but the poor mothers could get no word of their boys. I believe one or two field postcards came last night, but we don't know yet if they are all safe, or to what extent they have suffered. One mother I went to see had three sons away. She had been hearing regularly from them twice a week, and now she has been twelve days without any news. You may imagine what an anxious heart she has. One little wife is quite cheery because her husband has had his arm fractured in two places. "That will keep him out of it for a month or two, and perhaps he'll not be able to hold a rifle again!" It is wonderful what folks are thankful for nowadays!'

A week later, on the 22nd March, the blow falls.

'I got a telegram from Ronald this morning saying that he leaves for the front at two o'clock. It came as a shock although I knew it had to come one day. One cannot quite prepare oneself for these things. He is not taking his men with him. He and another captain and three lieutenants have been called up, I expect to fill the places of those who have been put out of action.

'I think the Camerons are having a rest now after fifteen days in the trenches, so I hope he will have a little preparation and rest before he has to face the enemy. I have always been proud of his height, but I could wish him rather more of the bantam now. His men seem to have done splendidly, but I don't think they were quite in the thick of things, so they have not lost so heavily as the Seaforths and Gordons. The officers have suffered more than the men.

'I got such a nice letter from him tonight, written after he had had his orders. It has done my heart good and helped a lot. I am glad he got his orders on Sunday when he had time to write a long kind letter'.

Father was welcomed by his Cameron men who had been withdrawn from the front line for a time. Allan had a bright idea for mitigating the rigours of active service. 'He asked me if we could send parcels to the men at the front. I said we could. "Well, I saw somewhere that the men at the front wanted mouth-organs. Do you think I could send one to Daddy? I could get one for a penny." Can you imagine Ronald sitting in a dug-out and trying to play a penny mouth-organ?'

April was uneventful, and Mother went south in May, leaving us in charge of kind gay Maggie Mathieson, with Mary the cook and Flora MacIntosh the young nursemaid. It must have been on the 18th or 19th of May that I and the two youngest children were dressing in the pink room, nurse Flora helping them with shoe-laces and back-buttons. Suddenly Maggie rushed in crying, 'They're all killed! All the boys are killed in the war!' She threw herself on the bed, weeping loudly. We stood paralysed, half-dressed; Flora and Peter holding their little clothes; I stunned by the window hearing her dreadful mourning. The news of Festubert had come to the Isle of Skye.

It was one of those murderous and futile engagements in which the outstanding courage of the men could only increase the carnage and disaster. A mile of German front-line trench had been captured and consolidated: on the 17th of May the Camerons with the Bedfords were ordered to attack the new German front and drive the enemy still further back. But to the right of this line was a redoubt bristling with machine-guns, and to the left a number of ruined houses also strongly held. No attempt had been made to explore or reconnoitre the ground to be covered, which the attackers found to be intersected with deep wide ditches. It was not even a forlorn hope: it was hopeless from the start.

The regimental history of the Queen's Own Cameron Highlanders describes the opening of the attack.

'After a fifteen-minute bombardment of the German trenches, the battalions advanced. Their attack was met by very heavy machine-gun fire, mainly from the redoubt, against the Bedfords and the right of the Camerons. So devastating indeed was the fire that were it not for the cover afforded by the gathering darkness not a man would have got across the open. D. Company lost all its officers and many of its men, but the survivors, rallied and led by C.S.M. William Ross of Portree, who displayed most conspicuous gallantry, continued to advance, and followed closely by C. Company, they captured their portion of the enemy position in dashing style, shouting their regimental cry as they sprang on the enemy with the bayonet'.

Father who was one of the officers of D. Company was dangerously wounded in the throat; only his amazing courage and self-control kept him from choking to death in the flow of blood. Sergeant-Major William Ross stayed by his side till help arrived, then he took command and heroically led the men forward.

But it was all in vain. Heavy rain fell during the night, filling the ditches and turning the land to mud. The Camerons, continually under fire from the redoubt, held their position through the darkness with only a handful of bombs, no machine-guns and no reserve ammunition. When day broke the Germans attacked with good supplies of grenades and ammunition, and the Camerons, outnumbered and abandoned, had to retire in broad daylight over a most difficult terrain, exposed to fire from both flanks. There were 231 casualties and brave William Ross was killed. He was not our gardener but another man of the same name, the village postman and shoemaker, father of five children, and over fifty when he went to the war. He was one of the noblest and most valiant even among so many of supreme courage. Portree will never forget his name.

John Buchan has described Festubert. 'It was an attempt to drive too narrow wedges into the enemy's front, and therefore predestined to failure. Like all struggles against odds it was fruitful in heroic deeds, like the performance of the 4th Camerons — Gaelic-speaking troops from Skye and the Outer Isles — who won the German line in darkness, and when forced out, came back like deer stalkers through the shell-holes and swollen ditches of that hideous No Man's Land'.

I remember the hush and dread that followed Maggie's anguish: we were desolate till Atten came to comfort us. We wept and said prayers together, and when news came that father was still alive even though wounded, we felt that our prayers had been answered. All Skye was mourning for lost fathers, husbands and sons, like Scotland after Flodden.

We were lucky to have Atten to look after us, for mother went straight up to London and visited father in the Camberwell General Hospital. He was in a small ward with a few other severely wounded officers: his bed was screened off and he had a bronchitis kettle steaming to help him breathe. He was not able to speak, and writing tired him, so she had to do most of the conversation, and felt envious when she heard the other patients chatting with their visitors. She saw him being fed through a tube, and thought it must be a very uninteresting way of having food.

But all through her life she had been gay and hopeful, and during her long stay she could see father making steady progress. 'The nurses say that he owes a great deal of his recovery to himself, they are quite surprised at the way he is getting on'. As the first shock of his wounding wore off he was able to get up for short periods and could talk in whispers. When she came back to Portree in July she felt sure that he would be able to come home in the not too distant future; we all looked forward to that happy day, and were reassured about the present. Mother wrote to him every day, and we all wrote on Sundays to the best of our ability.

He was pleased to hear that Alasdair and I had been doing well at school. Alasdair had passed his Qualifying Examination — the equivalent of the eleven-plus — at nine years old, though his tenth birthday came at the beginning of August. I had passed this examination the year before, at ten

Elizabeth Macdonald, taken during her engagement or soon after her marriage. She is wearing a Macdonald Clan brooch.

rising eleven, so I had had a year in the secondary division of the school, studying new subjects like French and Science under different teachers instead of being taught by the same person for a whole year or even two. For the first time we had regular examinations at the end of the year; mother used to complain that lower down in the school she had no way of estimating her children's progress. On a unique occasion we were given a test in arithmetic to see if we were ready to enter the Qualifying class: when she eagerly asked me about my result I reported cheerfully that I was 'second worst of the good ones', and she had to be content with that. But now I had come out first in French, English and Geography, and second in Mathematics, which was not supposed to be a strong subject, so there was good news to send to London.

Grannie in Paisley showed her appreciation of our success by sending a postal-order, and it is interesting to see that in these days two children could be rewarded and three more made happy, all for the sum of five shillings (25p). 'I am going to give 1/6d to the two older children, 1/- to the middle one, and 6d to the two wee ones, and let them spend it if they want to, or if they prefer, keep it in their banks till they think of something. There will be great consultation of catalogues when the boys come home'.

For Alasdair and Allan had gone off in the mail-motor to Glenhinisdale early in July — 'two happy and excited boys with a bag containing their worldly goods and two fishing-rods about three times their own size'. Flora, Peter and I, left at home during that sunny month of our last summer in Skye enjoyed each other's company. There were picnics in a favourite place by the stream that flowed from the first Storr loch into the town reservoir, then down by rock and moorland to be divided into the Scorrybreck burn and the lade that flowed towards the water-mill where oats were ground into meal. Foxgloves grew among the rocks near our special place, and there were spears of yellow iris among rushes and bracken where a tributary runlet welled through the peat; mats of wild thyme hung above the rushing water, and pink marsh heather and the gold-brown spikes of bog asphodel covered the uplands towards the stone-piled mass of a Pictish fort. Mother describes one afternoon.

'Last week we had two happy picnic teas in our pretty corner below the reservoir. Catriona was with us one time, and a little friend of Isobel's yesterday. Isobel and Flora took bathing-suits and bathed in the deep pool under the waterfall. Peter had his trousers off all the time, so had nothing to get wet below the waist. Isobel's friend fell in twice, and Isobel cut her foot, but what picnic is complete without a few such incidents? They all ate twice as much as they do indoors, and came home very happy and very untidy about seven o'clock'.

Then she tells of our happiness together. 'I am enjoying my small family; they are such darlings, and happy as the day is long. Isobel is so good to the wee ones; she never seems to want any other playmate than Flora although there are so many years between them, and they are both fond of Peter.

They sit in the upper branches of the pear tree where they have made a house for themselves, decorated with pots of growing pansies. Even Peter has been taught to climb to the very top, where his blue sailor collar appears among the leaves like a bit of blue sky. Isobel wrote a poem up there which she is going to dedicate, with another one on a waterfall, to Daddy, and send them to him for a birthday present. I am sure he will like them'.

Flora and I at seven and eleven years old were growing closer to each other. She was quieter than the rest of the family, but had a sweet little sense of humour and was an affectionate nestling child. I loved to read her my favourite poems, *The Ancient Mariner*, *The High Tide on the Coast of Lincolnshire*, *The Sacrifice of Er-Heb*, or the Scottish ballads as we curled up together in father's big chair with her head on my shoulders, or I would hold her in one arm as we lay under the huge sycamore tree in the graveyard where the long grass met the branches, and the sun glinted down on to the pages of *Alice in Wonderland*. Sometimes we went scrambling along the shore track towards Beal Point and had little picnics. She did not enter into my fantasy-life of adventures and princesses, but we shared long funny inventions about small gnomish people and a wizard who tried to control them, but was very absent-minded and always getting into trouble.

Mother was wrestling with our large garden; our worthless gardener had been dismissed, and she was trying to manage it herself with the help of a boy who ran away to go to sea.

'Little Johnnie, my garden-boy, page and general handy-man walked off the other morning. I had taken him to task for playing instead of working, which, being only fourteen, he much preferred, and he was deeply offended, so when he got the offer of a place as a cabin-boy on the steamer he jumped at it. The wages are 17/6d and all his food; 10/- wage and 7/6d extra for war risks, so it compares very favourably with my place and wage. I am going to do without a boy for the present; it's too much bother to look after them. I shall try to do a little gardening myself to keep things decent. If Ronald is not coming home for a while it will not matter so much'.

It was certainly good pay for a boy of fourteen, and it would have seemed more of a man's job to cruise to and fro on a MacBrayne boat that to do chores for the Bank House. But the garden was in a sorry plight. 'There are very few blackcurrants, and the vegetables are nearly all a failure, thanks to Harrison's incompetence and the incursions of sheep. I wish I had all I have put out this year on wages, manure and seeds back in hard cash again. I could then look the weeds calmly in the face, but it is provoking to pay for a well-filled garden and get nothing but weeds and worry'.

At the beginning of August mother took her remaining three and Maggie Mathieson to Glenhinisdale in a large hired car. She describes the reunion on the main road, two miles from the house. 'When we came to the bridge at the foot of the Glen we found two laddies in khaki shirts and red ties, and a wee lass in a blue dress waiting for us, all with bare feet — Alasdair, Allan and Trionag. They scrambled into the motor and we went merrily up the glen. How glad I was to see my laddies again, and how nice they looked — Alasdair with his honest smile showing all his big teeth, and Allan's blue eyes shining like stars out of his freckled face. We had a merry tea and a walk all over the place to see where the hay was cut, where the big potatoes were, where the ground was being reclaimed, and the new hen-run that Alasdair had been helping Uncle Norman to make. All too soon it was time to go home'

August went on peacefully with gardening and jam-making. Father had an operation on his throat which did not help as much as he had hoped; he wrote cheerfully on the whole, though from time to time he became depressed at his slow progress. Uncle George who visited him as often as he could and sent frequent reports said that these fits of depression were to be expected in a long illness and need not be taken too seriously, as on the whole he was improving; so mother wrote him letters full of sympathy and encouragement. The house began to seem strange without children or husband. 'I feel like Mariana in the Moated Grange, though I am not a-weary, a-weary, but enjoying the rest and quiet. Besides, my moated grange has no mouldering wainscots but is wonderfully spick and span. I can't get used to its tidiness and cleanness. It seems unnatural to go into the bathroom and find the towels all neatly folded and the floor and basin dry. Perhaps it is the silence that makes me feel like Mariana. You can't imagine the National Bank House without a sound!'

Towards the end of August she began to feel that she had had enough of this unnatural silence and tidiness, and that it would be pleasant to see her family again. 'After all, they are nice wee things, even though they turn the house upside down, and don't put away their toys, and make a racket, and forget their table manners, and kick the toes out of their boots and the heels out of their stockings, and work through the seats of their trousers in miraculously short time. One forgets these things when they are calling "Mama! Mama!" all at once, and crowding round to be kissed and hugged as I know they will be on Wednesday'.

So at the last possible moment we were collected and brought back to Portree to be civilised in time for school. 'Catriona and I went down for the children in a big motor. Long before we reached the bridge at the foot of the glen we were met by the whole six of them, looking like a small flock of sheep at the side of the road. They scrambled into the motor, and we had a jolly ride up the glen. They all looked brown and healthy; Alasdair and Flora have grown fat, Isobel has grown long, and Allan is covered with freckles. They were very sorry to leave the glen, except Peter, strangely enough, who wanted to go home with Mama. However when they were halfway there their thoughts began to turn with pleasant anticipation to home and their own things. We arrived after seven on Wednesday and they were all at school on Thursday morning, so there was a hurry-scurry, getting nails cut and garters made and suspenders repaired, and books and bags looked over and pencils given out, and baths all round, and boots and shoes looked to and new braces produced and collar studs unearthed, and a general brushing and polishing of each child. The result was highly satisfactory, and I felt proud of the tidy healthy little flock that went off so cheerily, Peter in a new sailor-suit, the two boys in their kilts, Isobel in her brown frock and Flora in a fresh print. It is lovely to have them back with all the noise and stir and chatter, and their stories of the Glen and school'.

At the beginning of October we had our autumn half-term holiday, the last of these times of freedom and happiness in the soft western air smelling of the sea, or of the moss and peat and bog myrtle of the moors. It was a fine day, and we had separate enjoyments. 'Isobel went with her little friend Nanette for a long walk to the further Storr loch, about seven miles away. They took pieces and had a glorious day among the moors and hills. Alasdair spent the forenoon gathering sphagnum moss and the afternoon out in a fishing-boat putting down nets. Allan spent the whole day on the pier trying to catch saithe. He brought none home but that did not matter; he was happy. When Flora and Peter saw the others going off on their adventures they wanted to go off too, so I gave them an apple and a piece each, and they went to the Black Rock and climbed to the top of the hill there. We all gathered at home for tea, and I bought 6d worth of cookies for a special treat'.

But father was still confined to an officer's ward in Camberwell General Hospital where he had been since May. Mother had given up her hopes of a speedy return to Skye; she realised that such a complicated wound needed more nursing care than it could have in Portree. But the hospital was not very comfortable for a slow prolonged convalescence; there was no fire in his ward, and no room where walking patients could sit. Autumn was drawing on, and there was danger that the fogs of a London winter would irritate his throat and produce coughing which might displace the trachea tube through which he breathed. His medical officer, Captain Harmer, wanted to send him to a south coast resort; Torquay was considered at first, but no hospital there was suitable; then Bath was spoken of, to father's disappointment, as he had been looking forward to living beside the sea again.

Finally it was decided to send him to Osborne House in the Isle of Wight, Queen Victoria's seaside home which was used as a convalescent hospital for officers. Towards the middle of October mother went south to visit him and go with him to his new quarters. For the last two weeks she had missed her regular reports from Uncle George who had gone to Edinburgh to be examined by specialists for long-standing abdominal trouble. An operation was advised, and while mother was in London news came that it had been unsuccessful and that her brother had died. We never knew this witty intelligent uncle who with mother was the liveliest of their family; a writer of clever teases and parodies in his letters home; a brilliant ophthalmic surgeon and a specialist of international reputation, whose death at thirty-nine was considered to be 'a serious loss to the science of ophthalmology in this country'. He was assistant surgeon at the Royal London Ophthalmic

Hospital and at St. Mary's Hospital, and had published papers on exudative retinitis so final and definitive that this condition became known as Coats' disease. From his obituary in the *Lancet* we learn: 'He was never happier than when thoroughly immersed in intricate pathological and histological work, and he had been heard to say that all he hoped from practice was to make enough to allow him to live and to devote the bulk of his time to the scientific work which was his greatest pleasure. He was one of the few ophthalmic surgeons who interested themselves seriously in comparative anatomy and pathology of the eye, and he spent much of his spare time in the Zoological Society's Gardens. Almost the last paper he read was on the Retina of the Fruit-eating Bat'. But I have only far-back memories of the flute and the burning-glass at Kildonan when I was seven years old. I also remember the imaginative interesting presents he sent me at Christmas; this bachelor uncle had an instinctive knowledge of what would please a little girl. There was a necklace of purple agates; a pair of blue velvet slippers folded into a case of the same material; and best present of all, my beloved green suede sling-bag which I always wore when I went on adventures among the Scorrybreck hazels or up the corries of Glenhinisdale. It could hold a pencil and notebook for writing poems, a pocket-copy of *The Ancient Mariner*, a tin cup for drinking spring-water, a buttered scone for long journeys, and on the way back a treasure-trove of crowberries or white heather.

The loss of their friend and brother was a tragic blow, a death in middle life after an operation is always unexpected, and one feels about an especially brilliant person that he must recover because the world cannot spare him. George's visits and his reports on progress had been invaluable to them both. The journey to Osborne was overshadowed by grief, though father was refreshed by the change of scene, and mother relieved to feel that he was away from the depressing atmosphere of a London hospital for seriously wounded men, and established comfortably within sight of the sea. She broke her journey at Paisley to spend some days with her family and share their sorrow; then in mid-November she set out for home. During the war the service to Portree via Mallaig was suspended, and travellers had to go the long way round by Inverness and Kyle of Lochalsh. Mother changed trains at Aviemore for Nairn where she spent the night with a friend who drove her to the station (probably in some kind of gig) to catch a train to Inverness that would connect with the Kyle train. But time-keeping on the Highland Railway was just as incalculable as it had been when we were coming home from Drumnadrochit.

'My train from Nairn was due to start at nine to catch the ten o'clock from Inverness. Time went on and the train did not come. When it did arrive it was almost ten o'clock. It is difficult to keep a philosophic calm when the time arrives for your train to leave and you are still many miles from the station, especially as missing it meant waiting a whole weekend for the next — even though you may have some knowledge of the ways of Highland trains. We got to Inverness at ten-thirty and I was relieved to find my train had not yet gone. I hurried to the luggage-office for my boxes, and found a seat — and waited and waited for two mortal hours before the train made up its mind to start. I was alone in the carriage till we came to Clunes about ten miles up the line, when a nice old farmer came in. He explained that he could not be bothered to wait till the train started in Inverness, so he had just walked on. When he came to the first station he was told that the train would not come for some time yet, so he walked on the next ten miles, and he was over seventy! I was very much amused: where would such things happen except in the Highlands?

'We did not leave Kyle till nearly five, and reached Portree shortly before nine! The sea was very rough; I stood it fairly well till we reached the headland outside Portree bay where it is always bad with a north wind, and then I succumbed within sight of home. However I was soon well again, and able to enjoy my supper. Isobel and Allan met me; Alasdair was afflicted with chilblains and the two wee ones were in bed, but wide awake and ready to give me a hearty welcome. We had a noisy supper, and it was ten o'clock before the bairns got to bed.

'Today it is again very cold with frost and snow, but I am glad to think of Ronald in the Isle of Wight. I hope it is milder there; at least he will have a cosy corner in his pretty room. I had a letter from him on Friday and already he feels the better for the change — eating and sleeping better and coughing less. He has been out on two days and has enjoyed it. I do hope the progress will continue'.

But only a month later, in the middle of December, before the slow improvement of health which was taking place in the mild climate of the Isle of Wight had time to be established, his medical officer had another idea. It was all meant for the best, but if he had been allowed to stay at Osborne he might eventually have returned to Skye.

'In Ronald's last letter he says there is talk of sending him to the south of France. They think he would make quicker progress there. Colonel Wardrup was going up to London and intended to see the War Office about it. The chief difficulty would be getting there, but they thought he might go in a hospital ship on its return journey to the Mediterranean from Southampton. I hate to think of him so far away, and I dread the journey for him, yet if it hurries up matters it would be a good thing. Meanwhile nothing is settled. They are very good to him at Osborne. Because he wasn't getting out much they have given him a large handsome sitting-room with two windows looking out to sea in addition to his bedroom. He was feeling pretty well when he wrote'.

Our last change of maids took place that December. Dear Maggie Mathieson went south to do war-time nursing, and Mary the cook also went off. All the children could now look after themselves, so only two maids were engaged, and they were both charming. Annie Stewart, the housemaid, was only eighteen; she was a pretty girl with gentle ways whom we all loved. She came to Glasgow with us when we left Skye and was with us there for a year.

Morag Mackenzie, the new cook, was twenty-one; she also was good-looking with dark hair and eyes and a clear rosy complexion.

By this time the war was having an effect on Hebridean transport and communications. The *Glencoe* made only three calls a week with the mails, and the cargo boats from Glasgow, instead of arriving regularly on Wednesdays and Saturdays, came to their piers as and when it suited them. Christmas Day in 1915 was a Saturday, but the Wednesday boat was still wandering among the Inner and Outer Isles, apparently with Santa Claus as a passenger. But our last Christmas in Skye was a climax of love and happiness.

'The Glasgow boat, which should arrive on Wednesday is not in *yet*. We can put no faith in boats nowadays; they come and go at their sweet wills, and bring your parcels or not as they feel disposed. I thought I was in good time to order my Christmas supplies by the Wednesday boat, with the result that when Christmas Eve came Santa Claus failed to keep his appointment. The younger children could not quite grasp the connection between Santa Claus and the Glasgow steamer, but I assured them that though he had made a little mistake about the day he would certainly come, so they are still hoping.

'We had a very happy Christmas all the same. Catriona came to breakfast at 8.30, and we had ham and eggs, a great treat nowadays when we only have tea and porridge as a rule. After breakfast we went up to the library where I had laid out their presents. Some books which Daddy ordered had not come, so the table was not so laden as usual, but there was enough to delight the bairns, who are not greedy. The girls were very pleased with a dolls' bed and some dolls' clothes; there were also new jig-saw puzzles, which were splendid as they had only childish ones before.

'The day was fine and mild, so the children went out while I prepared the Christmas feast. I thought we would have a light coffee-lunch at one, and not have dinner till five, when we could have it by lamp and candlelight and make it more of a festival. Some of the things such as fruit and cream were in the wretched Glasgow boat, but Lady Macdonald had given Alasdair a box of crackers, and they came in for decorations. We had delicious chicken soup, then roast duck and boiled fowl (both presents), then plum pudding and jellies and some chocolates, so we did not so badly. After dinner we had games — musical chairs and spin-the-plate — then Atten and I acted a charade, which was quite a new thing for them. The children were so happy and shrieked with delight. After the two wee ones went to bed we gathered round the fire and Isobel read us some of her latest stories; at eight we had tea and the bigger ones went to bed, and Atten and I had a chat over the fire till 9.30 when the party was over. It was a very happy evening, and the absent Daddy was not forgotten either in heart or in speech. We are all hopeful that we may have our own dear Father Christmas with us next Christmas-tide'.

1916: The Cruel Distance

In 1915 we had been compelled to go to school on Christmas Day, an edict of the School Board which shocked us by its tyranny, but in 1916 New Year's Day was just as festive as Christmas. Both were on Saturdays, and Santa Claus had at last arrived by the Glasgow boat. Children who live in houses where light comes on at the touch of a finger do not know the excitement of groping in the dark for a long black stocking of knitted wool, and trying to guess what it contained by feeling it over. Then the lamp would be carried in, sending its soft glow round the shadow of the opened door, and at last we would *see*.

'Both my new maids are doing well. To show you how willing they are, I told them to do their morning work particularly well on New Year's morning, so as to have everything nice if visitors called. They got up at 5.20! As they were coming downstairs at 5.30 they were greeted by a chorus of "Happy New Year!" Every child was awake, for Santa Claus had paid his postponed visit, and they were all eager for lamps to be lighted and investigations made. A good many of the contents of their stockings were disposed of before breakfast, yet they were all hungry at 8.30.

'Catriona came again to breakfast and spent the day. It was wet and miserable, so it had to be spent indoors, but there were many interesting preparations for dinner to be made, so they all gave a hand and were happy. We had it at five o'clock again, with mulligatawny soup, roast pheasants, apricot tart, trifle and jelly, crackers and sweets. Then the three older ones entertained us by acting charades; they were very amusing. We had musical chairs and games for the wee ones till they went to bed. Atten had brought down the *Students' Song Book* which was new to the bairns, so we introduced them to some lively choruses. It made me feel young again to shout "Polly-wolly-doodle" and "John Peel". Then we all had tea with cake and shortbread'.

But a combined intercessory service of the Established and U.F. churches that was celebrated on the following day left her feeling very cross. 'Mr. Black was the preacher, and he took for his text Joshua commanding the sun and moon to stand still, and spent most of his time giving the arguments for and against the possibility of this miracle; then he ended up with all the arguments justifying the wiping out of the Caananites by the Children of Israel, men, women and children. It was all so far from the point, and so uninspiring and tiresome. One came away feeling that whether the sun stood still or not was a matter of very little importance today, as it would not be likely to suggest itself as a way out of a difficulty to any of our modern

Joshuas, and if the Israelites were so wise when they slew the women and children, the Germans were not much to blame when they followed their example'.

The news of father continued to be good. 'He seems really to be making progress, especially since he got his fine sitting-room. He was able to enjoy turkey and plum pudding on Christmas Day, and seems altogether more comfortable. It is very cheering'.

But in the middle of January the fatal decision was taken, and he was uprooted from Osborne where he had settled down and was gradually recovering, and sent to the south of France. No trouble or expense was spared over the journey; it is tragic to think that the whole plan was a mistake. The news came suddenly, and mother tried as usual to look on the bright side. 'I am trying to be glad about it, but I can't help feeling anxious till I know he is safely there, and comfortable, and in good hands. It is a long way off but it is good to think there will be lots of sunshine, and he can go out and about, and probably recover even more quickly than he could in the Isle of Wight. He is sorry to leave his comfortable quarters and kind friends at Osborne and go out again into the unknown, but he was feeling much stronger, and better able to face the long journey. I wonder how long it will take for an answer to a letter to come from Mentone to Portree — nearly a fortnight, I should think. It takes a week to get a letter from Osborne'.

The long delay in receiving letters was a cause of great anxiety when he became seriously ill. Next week there is an interesting account of the journey as far as Paris. The decision to send him was inconsiderately sudden and peremptory, but the arrangements made were luxurious enough for an invalid millionaire. His uniform had been covered with blood and abandoned after the battle, so it was unintelligent to think that he could all at once produce one after spending months in hospital clothes.

'Ronald had a telegram from the War Office saying he was to leave next day, then followed a letter saying he must have a passport and travel in uniform. Colonel Wardrop telephoned to the War Office that he had no uniform and that there did not seem time to get a passport. After a lot of trouble they said that a greatcoat and cap would be accepted as sufficient uniform, but that a passport was absolutely necessary. This involved a photograph, and Ronald had none. He was to leave at one o'clock but the Colonel took a photograph that morning and somehow or other got it done in time — someone would have to hustle, I should think! On Thursday they went to London and stayed at the Hotel Cecil where of course they had every comfort; there they met a doctor and nurse who had been sent from Netley to conduct him to France. On Friday the doctor rushed around seeing about passports etc, and in the evening they went to Folkestone where they stayed all Friday night. They were told to be on the steamer at 8.45 to secure a deck-cabin which was to be reserved for them. They were there in good time, but the boat did not leave till 4.10 a.m. so they had seven hours to wait; however he was well wrapped up and did not feel the cold. The crossing was the part of the journey he dreaded most, as he did not know what would happen if he got sick, but it was perfectly calm and he crossed comfortably'.

They spent Saturday night at Boulogne and went on to Paris on Sunday. There they were met by a wonderfully fine motor car — 'the last word in magnificence and comfort. Indeed it seemed to be all silver and brocade, and to have the contents of several dressing-cases stuck round the tonneau'. From the time they landed in France they were in the charge of the Red Cross Society, and were very well looked after. In the Paris hotel Ronald and his nurse had a suite of rooms with a bathroom to themselves.

'They stayed in Paris for Sunday night and Monday, and when he wrote he expected to travel south on Monday night. Sleeping compartments had been engaged, and they would not get up till they arrived at Marseilles on Tuesday morning. He was feeling well when he wrote, and quite enjoying the journey. The nurse, he said, was "a treasure". I think he is meeting too many nice nurses; I am getting a little jealous. I am longing to hear how he got on for the rest of the journey, and how he is settling down in Mentone'.

He arrived in Mentone on the 18th of January, and his first letter reached Portree sometime before the 30th. It sounded cheerful and encouraging. 'Ronald is delighted with Mentone. There is bright sunshine from 7.30 till 3.30, lovely flowers, and oranges growing on the trees. The hotel where he is staying is only partly converted into an Officers' Home. There are about ten officers, and the rest of the hotel goes on as usual. It is connected with the Red Cross. It has just been opened, and there is only a matron and one nurse. He had a very nice room, but was to be moved to a larger one with a large verandah. It amuses me very much — wherever Ronald goes they at once want to give him a bigger room or add to his comfort in some way. There is a motor car which has been provided by the farmers of Dorsetshire, and he had a delightful drive with the nurse. There is no resident doctor, but one visits every day. He thoroughly examined Ronald when he arrived, and found the lungs wonderfully clear, with no trace of bronchitis; the discharge and cough seem all to come from the trachea. He has had the outer tube changed once, and as always happens when he is in new hands he suffered a good deal, but I hope they will soon get used to his ways. I was wondering how he would do for books, but he writes that there is an English library in the place and he has joined it. Only he and another officer need attention during the night, and the nurse sleeps in a room between them, opening into both. I think he will be happy there; his letters are most interesting and cheerful'.

So the man of Skye who loved the brown rush of the Glenhinisdale river and the bold sweep of the cliffs enclosing Portree bay, and the jagged line of Cuillin against the sunset, tried to settle down among the palms and mimosa of Mentone. A week later another letter has been received. 'Ronald has a motor run every day with the matron or a nurse; a new nurse has come, so now there are two as well as the matron. I expect the new nurse was on his account; he needs so much attention both night and day. It is wonderful how much has been done for him; he tells me that the doctor and nurse were sent from Netley just to convey him to the Riviera; they waited there for two days to see him comfortably settled and then returned to Netley. He does not seem to walk about much, but just sits on his balcony all day except when he is out in the motor. I don't think there is much improvement yet, and he always suffers a good deal when he changes hands. He has to be careful not to sit out too late in the afternoon as the evenings are cold. I do hope he will soon feel better and be able to go about with freedom'.

Next week mother is becoming a little uneasy; he seems to have no energy for walks, which he had enjoyed at Osborne, and he is reluctant to give much account of his feelings or his surroundings. It is as if his longing and homesickness were so deep that he was unable to interest himself in this foreign place, or to describe how he felt for fear of losing courage. 'Ronald's last two letters have been disappointing in this way; he has filled them with comments on *my* letters instead of with news of his doings and feelings. He has had the first rain since his arrival, and seemed to enjoy a day in the house. I cannot tell you why he does not walk about. It puzzles me too. He *may* go out for walks, but he does not mention them; he only speaks of lying on his verandah and going for motor-runs'.

Meanwhile family life went on as usual. After her late start Flora was getting on well at school, though the subject set for composition seems rather weighty for a seven-year-old. 'Flora has just moved to a higher class where they have essays to do at home. She announced that she had to write an essay on Robert Clive, then she added wistfully, "I was hoping it would be about a mouse, for I know a good deal more about a mouse than I do about Robert Clive". The poor wee smout! I am sure she does. Allan had an essay to do on what he called in its heading his "Otebeografrae". Isn't it a lovely word?'

An epidemic of whooping cough broke out among the younger children in Portree, and Peter became ill, though not seriously; he was always a strong lively little boy. Another patient was our cousin Angus, son of father's brother Donald, a handsome lad in his mid-teens who lived with relations at Penefieler across the bay and was beginning his apprenticeship at the bank. He stayed with us if the weather was bad or he was not well, so at this time he was with us for several weeks. We admired him very much, and felt as if we had acquired an elder brother.

In February one of the tall crowded tenement houses in Portree's main street was burned down, an alarming disaster in that season of long darkness with no local fire-service available. Mother writes on Sunday the 20th: 'We have had a sad tragedy here today. About five o'clock this morning a large tenement in Wentworth Street took fire and was completey gutted. Fortunately a patrol-boat was in the bay, and the sailors came on shore and did splendid service, otherwise the whole street would have been burnt. As it is one woman has lost her life. She had a little shop on the ground floor, and she has been drinking lately; the fire is supposed to have started in her room.

The house was occupied by poor decent families, and several of the scholars and motor-men stayed there as lodgers. They were all turned out into the street at five in the morning, most of them in their night-attire or with a garment or two hastily snatched up; none of them saved any of their belongings. They were lodged for the time being in the Portree Hotel, and have been taken in by friends or neighbours.

'I have been busy today gathering what clothes I can spare to help them, and I have made two good big bundles. I expect they will be given plenty of clothes, but where they will find homes I don't know, and of course none of them had their furniture insured so they lost everything. "Even the watch under my pillow!" as one man was lamenting. Another man was congratulating himself that his week's pay was in his trouser-pocket and he had managed to put on his trousers. He had a wife and several children, and nothing else that they had was saved'.

A week later the whole community was trying to help the poor families who had lost their homes. A collection was made which raised more than £50, a substantial sum in these days; there was also a collection in the school to buy books for the scholars who had lost their possessions. The stone walls of the house, burned down to the basement inside, stood with charred empty window-frames in Wentworth Street, a place of horrid fascination to Allan, who had plenty of time to gaze, since the junior school had closed because of whooping-cough.

'The poor people who were burnt out of home last Sunday are settling down here and there. Some have managed to find rooms and others are still with friends. We have done our best to get clothes for them, and some sort of furniture to go on with. I gave my chair-bed to one family. I took some clothes I had made to another family on Tuesday afternoon; I found the two wee girls still in bed for want of clothes, but all quite happy, so thankful that they had escaped and that none of the children had taken cold. It was a miracle that they did escape; five minutes more and none of them would have been saved as the stair was on fire when they came down. They did not find the remains of the poor woman who lost her life till Wednesday. They found some queer things; a purse with £20 in paper and another with £2 in silver which somehow managed to escape the flames. Allan went to watch every morning, and came home with weird tales of the things that had been turned up in the ruins'.

The two younger children's birthdays which came so close together were still festive occasions. 'Flora's birthday was enjoyed by us all. Isobel was up early, and had a crown of ivy made and the table decorated by breakfast-time. There were a good many small parcels round her plate, so she was a very happy little girl. The morning post brought a box of cakes and tarts from Aunt Mary which gave us a proper birthday dinner and tea, and it also brought the two new records Jeanie sent us. I kept these for a surprise; we had Catriona to tea, and afterwards a concert with our new records — the *Faust* ballet-music and the *Zampa* and *Poet and Peasant* overtures'.

Peter also had a happy birthday in spite of his whooping-cough. 'Thank you all for your birthday gifts to my wee Peter. There are few toys to be had in Portree, fewer than ever since the war, but we managed to procure four sixpenny toys which with Auntie's book and your postal-order made a brave show on the breakfast-table. He is still whooping away, but Angus who is staying with us is much better'.

But letters from father were disquieting. Instead of encouraging his wound to heal naturally the doctor at Mentone was experimenting with treatment which sounds both amateurish and drastic. 'He is being dosed with pills to dry up the mucus, and is having the trachea deluged four or five times a day with some disinfecting oil. At first he was given cocaine to deaden the parts, but he thought that gave him headaches and took away his appetite, so it was stopped, but without the cocaine the treatment brings on fits of coughing. He is finding it all rather depressing, especially as he does not feel it is doing him much good'.

And during these early spring months letters from the distant Riviera were travelling more and more slowly. To reach Inverness the ageing locomotives of the Highland Railway had to climb 1484 feet over the Pass of Drumochter between Pitlochry and Aviemore; then the mails had another long haul across the moors of Ross-shire, reaching Kyle of Lochalsh late in the afternoon. There on three days a week they were transferred to the *Glencoe* which paddled doggedly round the coast of Skye, its obsolete steeple-engine wheezing up and down on the deck. Mother writes rather bitterly to her relations who thought they were enduring hardship when deliveries of mail were reduced to two a day.

'I wish *our* postal deliveries could be curtailed to *only* two a day! Ours are only on three days a week, and besides that, the boat has been arriving later and later, often not till ten o'clock. If this happens I don't get my letters till the *next* day, or if I am very anxious for them I have to keep a girl up till eleven or after, and send her to the post-office to fetch them. I did this on Friday, as I was dying to hear from Ronald and had not had a letter all week. His letter was a little more cheerful, but not so much as I would like. He is still having his motor drives and is out from two to two and a half hours, but he does not go for walks except occasionally in the garden. He does not say why. He has taken it into his head to write home only once a week, so I feel half-starved. It is so unlike him. Before I have put his letter back into its envelope I am longing for the next. I am going to tell him that I must have a letter at least twice a week so long as he is an invalid, however short it is. He says nothing of the treatment this week, so I don't know whether he is still having it. I have written to the Matron to ask her how she thinks he is getting on. I feel I want an outside opinion, for the patient is not always the best judge of his own condition'.

On March 5th there had been complete loss of contact for more than a week. Apparently the naval patrol vessels that quested to and fro among the Hebrides for submarine bases or enemy communications supplemented the

Glencoe's efforts to bring mail to Portree as well as helping to extinguish fires: this one must have arrived on a Saturday night.

'I am sorry to say I have no news at all to give you of Ronald. I have had no letter since the Friday before last. You can imagine how I am longing for news. Fortunately a patrol boat came in late last night bringing mails. I sent the girls over to the post-office last night, and Angus between nine and ten this morning, but the mails had not been sorted, so I cannot tell whether there is one for me or not. Most likely there will be, unless it has been delayed somewhere, for I am sure he would not leave me ten days without news when he knows how anxious I am'.

Probably strict Sabbatarian principles forbade the sorting of mail on a Sunday, no matter how anxiously letters were being longed for, but it does seem hard that she should have to wait another day for news that she could have had earlier. The suspense and silence must have been even worse than news that was not too good. She writes on Monday evening.

'I got a short letter tonight; it was just as I feared; Ronald has not been very well. The weather was wet and cold, and he caught a chill and had a slight return of the trouble he had in London in October, though not such a bad attack. He was still in bed when he wrote, as the weather was still cold and wet, but he hopes to be better soon. Meanwhile the treatment has been abandoned. Fortunately he is in the sunshine of the Riviera with the summer before him and not in the fogs of London, so I hope he may soon begin really to improve'.

Still she was hoping for the best and looking on the bright side. On the 8th of March a letter arrived from the matron, so at last she had an objective view of the case, like the welcome reports which George had sent her from London. The matron was called Mabel Anderson, and sounds an able and kind-hearted woman. She writes first about her patient's setback. 'He has had a little pleurisy following on some congestion caused probably by a particle of food entering the trachea in a fit of coughing. We hope that in a day or two this may clear up, but he has had some rise of temperature, and of course has had to be kept in bed'.

Then she goes on to describe his general condition. 'He had decidedly improved in regard to his wounds and the condition of the trachea, also in general health. He is very nervous about himself, which is natural considering all he has been through, but if we could rouse him more and get him to go out often, he would probably mend faster. We have had a week of rain, which is against him, but we hope when the sun returns and the air is clear and dry again he will speedily pick up lost ground'.

Evidently she was concerned about his languor, and could sense the deep loneliness which his courage was pressing into silence, for in the next paragraph she suggested the obvious remedy, as it seemed to her.

'I know it is difficult for you to leave home, but if you could manage it I am sure Lady Dudley would be willing to pay your expenses out and while you are here. It must be very trying for you to be so far away while he is so helpless, and I wish I had not to report this setback'.

It was a kind and sympathetic letter; her heart longed to follow its suggestion, but the matron did not realise how difficult it would be for poor mother to travel all the way from the inner Hebrides to the south of France in war-time conditions, nor how many complicated arrangements would have to be made before she could leave at all. Five children, one of them with whooping-cough, had to be placed in the care of friends or relations, as the maids were too young to be left for six weeks or more in charge of a family whose parents could not be reached in an emergency. The letters that follow show her longing to be with her husband if she could help him in any way, and her troubled sense of the great difficulties involved. I do not know why the problem could not have been solved by Aunt Agnes coming to Skye and keeping house for us till mother returned; it would seem to be an obvious piece of helpfulness from an unmarried aunt living at home without any special duties. She did offer to come, but apparently with some reluctance, and mother wanted to accept her offer but felt it might be taking undue advantage. In the end Ronald forbade her to come; it was a relief at the time, but it meant that she never saw him again.

As soon as she had read the matron's letter she wrote to her sister Mary, the wisest and most level-headed of the family. 'It is about her suggestion that I should come out that I need your advice. You can understand how torn I am by desire to go if I can be of any use or comfort to Ronald, and how it seems almost impossible to surmount the obstacles in the way. It would take about a fortnight to come and go from here to Mentone, and I would have to stay for a week or two there if I were to do any good. My girls are so young to leave in charge, and the children are constantly needing clothes made and mended; I cannot see how I can leave them for so long. I might get the three older ones boarded out and leave the two wee ones with the girls, that it the only thing I can think of for the meantime'.

Two days later, on the 10th of March, she had time to think things over, and it seemed to her that she could not leave her responsibilities behind and go on a such a long expensive journey without obtaining Ronald's consent. From her letters it can be seen that she was a very energetic and lively character, but Ronald was the head of the house: he had the last word in any important decision, and it might have done more harm than good if she had appeared at his bedside in Mentone without any warning. So she had written, telling of her suggested arrangements, and asking him to telegraph if he would like her to come. It would be a warm and comforting letter, making light of difficulties and eager to be with him again.

She ran over possible schemes in a letter to Aunt Agnes; it would probably be better to close the house and disperse the family. 'I would like the older ones to continue at school if possible. Catriona says she is willing to take Isobel. I am going to ask Mrs Mackenzie who lives in the house beside the pier if she would take the boys. Her husband is the Sunday School superintendent, and she was a nurse in the Sick Children's hospital; they are both fond of children and fond of our boys. Of course I would pay board for them and for Isobel.

'Then for the wee ones. There is the difficulty of Peter's whooping-cough, but it is almost better now. I would like to send him to the Glen if they do not object. His wee sister has not had it, but I don't think there would be much risk of infection by then. If it would be convenient to you I could bring Flora with me and leave her in Hayfield till I come back. She is a contented quiet wee mouse and can look after herself; I don't think she would be much trouble to you.

'I have also written to Lady Dudley, asking her if there is any arrangement to allow wounded officers' wives to travel at a reduced rate when visiting their husbands, and if there is any accommodation I could get at Mentone, also if there are any Red Cross places where I could stay on the way. I am writing about my passport so as to have everything ready if Ronald wants me to come. There are a frightful lot of things to think about. It is not easy to get the children all decent for their new homes — Flora is hardly respectable at present!'

On Sunday the 12th of March she had a telegram from Aunt Agnes offering to come and keep house. At first she was delighted, especially as, on thinking things over, she had been wondering whether a still-whooping Peter would be very welcome at Glenhinisdale. 'I know they would do anything to help me, but they have a holy terror in these glens of anything infectious, and the school-teacher stays with Grannie. If the folks think Peter has whooping-cough it is likely that not a child will come to school. The teacher herself has not had it, and would not come up to Portree in case she might catch it. Peter is nearly better, but he still coughs and whoops'.

But on Monday a letter arrived from Aunt Agnes which sounded more half-hearted than her telegram. 'I see that it would not be easy for you to get away'. Perhaps it would be better after all to disperse the children especially as she had heard from the Glen and they were willing to take both the younger ones, showing a noble disregard for possible infection. The kind Mackenzies too had offered to take Flora and Peter as well as the two boys — 'he seemed quite taken with the idea of having them'. They were young married people, very fond of children, who had lost their first baby, and seemed pleased with the idea of a ready-made temporary family.

Then on Wednesday the 15th of March she had a lengthy and decisive telegram from father. Her letter, probably written on the 9th, must have travelled very quickly to Mentone. 'He thinks my coming utterly out of the question. He says: "For one thing you could not possibly be here until the beginning of April, when I trust I shall be leaving for England. No one stays here during the whole of April. The journey would take you ten or twelve days, and the idea of breaking up the home and sending the children here and there is to me utterly distasteful. Please don't think of it any more"'.

What a relief! If he was coming home so soon she could look forward to visiting him in England, perhaps taking Isobel with her. No need to close the house and scatter the children, and set out on a long journey into the unknown. However it seemed rather odd that so much trouble had been taken to send him so far away if he was coming home in April. She did not realise that the idea was wishful thinking: if the Riviera was too hot in April for anyone to stay there, he would have to endure only one more month of exile. On the same day a letter came from the matron: he was to be removed from the convalescent hotel in Mentone to a military hospital in Marseilles.

There had also been a kind letter from the secretary of Lady Dudley who managed a fund for helping wounded officers' wives to visit their husbands: it seems to have been run in a friendly personal way without any red tape or form-filling. 'Lady Dudley wishes me to tell you that she will be very pleased to arrange for you to join Captain Macdonald at Mentone, and to meet the expense of your journey and your accommodation while you are out there. Will you kindly let us know when you wish to go? It will be necessary for you to call here with reference to your passport and journey. It would therefore be advisable for you to be in London for at least one day before you start for Mentone'. How generous and helpful! — they would have taken care of all her problems. But how glad she was that she need not set out after all.

Early in April father wrote from Marseilles saying that he was making good progress in his new quarters. 'The hospital is in a French château and is fairly comfortable. I have a room to myself. There is a balcony and the place is surrounded by pine woods. It is about three and a half miles from the Marseilles station, but the city comes up quite close to it. There are only about seven officers at present, but 150 men. These are mainly Indians of the Lahore division, but they are leaving soon, and then I believe we are to have Australians. I took my food well today, though it is not equal to the food at Mentone'.

Family cares came back into the foreground. Alasdair's eyes were not all they should be; his teachers had noticed that he could not see the blackboard properly, and when she gave him a rough test she found that he could not see at a distance nearly so well as Angus or Allan. She would have to send him south in the Easter holidays to an oculist, but she did not want to leave Skye herself till father came back to England. She decided to send both boys to keep each other company, and to ask one of the teachers from Portree school to escort them. There is a glimpse of the difficulties of travel from the island during the war. 'I could not let them go south alone, as it is a complicated journey even for more experienced travellers. You have to take one ticket on the boat, another at Kyle. You must see that your luggage is labelled at Kyle or it won't be put on the train. Then you generally have to change both at Inverness and at Perth'. In the end they travelled with a lively Irish woman who taught us physics and chemistry and was going home by Glasgow; during the journey she lit a cigarette, and they gazed at her with wide-eyed wonder. When they came back they were put into the Inverness train and met by Allan's wee Annie, now a wife and a mother, who took them home for the night and sent them off in the Kyle of Lochalsh train next morning.

But all the time there was an undertone of disquiet, a feeling that Ronald might be needing her, and that she should go as soon as it could be arranged. April was passing without any word of his coming home. He did not seem to be very well although they both tried to be cheerful. 'He has had the outer tube changed for the first time at Marseilles. It was an ordeal, but not so bad as the first two times at Mentone. There have also been two days of the "Mistral", a cold trying wind which everyone hates on the Riviera, so he has been confined to his room, but when he wrote he was sitting out on his balcony again. He says he is improving but still feels very weak and languid. Perhaps he may feel the benefits of the Riviera more when he gets back to this country'.

So the letters end, with poor mother torn between care for her children in Skye and anxiety for her husband in the south of France. It was a cruel distance; the journey in wartime would probably have taken a week of slow complicated travel. Indeed the decision to send our father there was an unfortunate one, though taken with the best intentions and carried out with every care. At that time coughs were still associated with cold; it was hoped that a cough, no matter what the cause, would be cured by sending the patient to a warmer climate, so that many consumptives (like Katherine Mansfield) were still going to Rome and to the south of France, though sanatoria in Switzerland like the one in *The Magic Mountain* were coming into favour. Father's cough was caused by his inflamed wound which now would have been cured by antibiotics: it might have healed gradually if he had been nursed in clean fresh air with absence of strain and anxiety. He was making good progress at Osborne which seems to have suited him very well, but this led his doctor to think that he would improve even faster on the Riviera. The long journey tired him out; the painful experimental treatment weakened him; the early spring weather at Mentone was changeable and trying, and worst of all must have been the distance from his native land, the deep inarticulate homesickness of the Highlander. One can see that he is losing heart: he lies on the balcony instead of going for walks; he comments on her news instead of describing his alien and unenjoyed surroundings; he writes only once a week as he becomes more and more weary. He must have longed for her cheerful loving presence, but he forbade her to come, to spare her the effort of the long journey and the scattering of his children into strange houses. At Marseilles the throat infection developed into pneumonia, and he died there in June 1916.

All through his year in hospital mother was steadily hopeful: she never doubted that in the end he would come back to his big chair in the library and everything would go on as before. His death was a blow from which she never quite recovered. Our tenure of the National Bank House came to an end; we left Skye for many years, and she took a flat in Glasgow so that we could go to schools there. The year 1916-1917 was one of the most difficult on the home front; food was becoming scarce, but rationing had not yet been imposed. She struggled on through a wet foggy winter in the rough dark Glasgow of wartime, sleeping badly and probably not eating enough so that her family could have more. A year after father's death she was found to have advanced tuberculosis: the flat was given up and she entered a sanatorium on Deeside for two years. We were boarded with our aunts in Paisley.

When I was told that we were not going back to Skye I wept myself into a stupor: I had never known such anguish. It was the final blow after father's death. Mother had taken Flora and me south with her and sent the boys to Glenhinisdale, but I had no idea that this was not a visit like so many previous ones, and that at the end of the summer we would not all go home. She broke the news to me in the spare-bedroom of our grandmother's house: she was going back to Portree to remove the furniture and bring the boys south, then we would all settle in Glasgow. It was an appalling shock. I clung to her in floods of tears and implored her to let me go back with her. The bitterest part of my grief was that I had not said goodbye to all the places by the sea or by the streams and woods that I loved as if they were people. I wanted to put my arms round every tree and kiss every rock before I left them. My agony must have been painful to mother who had enough heartbreak to bear. She was gentle but firm: to go back with her would make it harder to leave again, and I must make up my mind to the parting now.

Perhaps poor little Peter suffered most from the break-up of our home. We at least were together, but he was left behind in Glenhinisdale: mother could not take him away from his father and sister, nor undertake the care of a child not hers on her widow's pension and allowances. But he was only six, and could not understand why he had been orphaned for a second time. 'She was the only mother I ever knew,' he said to me years later, and he described his feeling of abandonment when he saw the car go down the glen taking Alasdair and Allan back to Portree and leaving him behind. 'Well, Peter, you're on your own now!' Uncle John had said: he was a kind man, and could not have realised how his casual remark would be remembered as underlining the desolation of the small inarticulate figure, bearing his pain silently as he had borne the dentist's mauling a year earlier. The child had accepted his natural place as the youngest of a family, to be petted and teased, and to share all the birthdays and holidays and treats; now he was torn up and had to struggle along in an environment that was much harder and harsher. He was sent to Glenhinisdale school where the teaching was in English even in the youngest classes, but where all the children spoke Gaelic among themselves, so that he was shut out from the playground games and mocked by his school-mates. Aunt Catriona was becoming more and more obsessed by the stern cruel Calvinism that was too common in Skye, and any inadvertent 'breaking of the Sabbath' was threatened with hell-fire. The little boy who had said so happily to mother, 'I was sitting on God's knee last night', lay terrified in his bed in case his Maker would destroy him for sliding on a frozen pool one Sunday afternoon. He must have felt that all the warmth and happiness and affection he had once known were going on somewhere and that for no fault of his own he had been shut out: he did not realise that we too were having a hard time under the unsympathetic discipline of our maiden aunts. He grieved that mother never came to see him, but after three years in sanatorium and nursing-home, when the illness was arrested, she was a permanent invalid, never leaving home and spending the winter in bed.

However we did have a home again, and our good Aunt Mary unselfishly gave up her post as matron in Largs to keep house and look after us. We lived in Kilmacolm, in the clean fresh air of the Renfrewshire moors, and mother's room was the centre in the house where she was always ready to hear news, sympathise and plan for her children. She was determined to give us the best possible education. I went to the Park School in Glasgow; Alasdair and Allan first to the Glasgow High School and then as Foundationers to Fettes College, Edinburgh. Somehow money was found and expenses covered for mother's hopes and ambitions. Before she died in 1928 I had graduated from Somerville College Oxford, helped by a grant from a fund for the education of women, especially of girls made fatherless by the war, while Alasdair won a scholarship and Allan a sizarship to St. Johns College, Cambridge. Eventually in 1943 Alasdair became house-master of Chatham House, Stowe, and then for a time was second master of that famous school, and he has written two books which record its history. Allan entered the Colonial Service, and after postings to Ceylon and Uganda was Colonial Secretary in Sierra Leone, and in 1956 Chairman of the Civil Service Commission in Nairobi. In 1965 he was sent to Aden to do similar work and ended his career dramatically by being ambushed and shot in the dark by an Arab gunman. He grappled with the man and was shot a second time, but recovered from two dangerous wounds, and was soon climbing mountains again. On leave from a teaching career, I wrote two novels, *The Fairy Hill* and *Love is too Young*, and a fiction-biography of Matthew Arnold from 1848 to 1852 called *The Buried Self.*

Flora, deeply in love, was happily married in 1930, but in 1939 she was found to have that tragic illness, multiple sclerosis, incurable and long lasting. She bore it with the greatest cheerfulness and courage, doing everything she could until the final years of helplessness, supported by the constant love and care of Graham Parker her husband. And although poor little Peter had to go through the shock of apparent desertion as a child, he had a happy life. He farmed his father's croft at Cuidrach and grandfather's at Glenhinisdale; his wife Chrisanna is a dear, and they had three fine children, Mary, Nancy and young Peter who still farms in Glenhinisdale. He was impulsive and affectionate with a great sense of humour. He died in 1977; it is strange that the two little ones, the nursery pair, have gone, while Alasdair, Allan and I, the big children, are still here.

I did not go back to Skye for many years, until I was earning money and could afford to travel. Then I stayed with Atten, once in summer and once in

January, and found everything as it had been. For Skye changes very little: its winged coastline of sea-loch and headland; its great stone hills rising from the shore to the clouds, are as they were when the Norsemen came south, their brawny arms straining at the oars, and their bulls-hide sails slanting to the northwest wind. They were the ancestors of Somerled, Lord of the Isles, and they scattered Scandinavian place-names over the island — Orbost, Totaig and our own Glenhinisdale. The history of Skye is obscure as if it wrapped itself in its own mists: tales of savage clan-battles and legends of sea-horses and fairy-women are caught in glimpses as the vapours clear and close again. A baby falls from his nurse's arms into the sea, and the cliff-fortress of Duntulm is abandoned: another baby is found wrapped in the Fairy Flag of Dunvegan: at Trumpan there is a massacre in a church, and at Castle Uisdean confused treachery. We know hardly anything of pre-Reformation Skye; according to Adamnan, St. Columba came there twice, and it shared the light that spread from Iona in the sixth century. But all the old churches dedicated to the Celtic saints, Kilbride, Kilchoan, Kilmuir and Kilmaluag have long ago fallen into ruin so that their stones are not to be distinguished from the stones of the hillside. The priest and the bell and the holy well are no more; we do not know whether their faith was put down with cruelty or allowed to die from lack of tending. The mist has come down again, and when it rises there is an emigrant ship in Portree bay and the Rev. Mr. McQueen is about to officiate in Erse.

In fact the annals of Skye are of geology rather than history: its events are the shaping of the Cuillins by Thor and Lok; the stroke that sheared the tops off Healaval Mhòr and Healaval Bheag, the splitting and erosion of wild pinnacles at the Storr and the Quirang, or in the sea off Idrigill Point where they are called Macleod's Maidens. Against these amazing landscapes human habitation is a melancholy strain, like the Gaelic chant of the Solitary Reaper. The kelp industry prospers and decays; there are clearances at Suisnish and Boreraig; fishing flourishes or is neglected. The black houses crouching low on the ground with thatched roof and tiny windows give way to comfortable dwellings of stone, but the crofts which covered the glens and loch-sides with a patchwork of small fields have become grazing-pasture, or are left to go back to moorland, so that only a shadow-pattern can be seen of the once carefully tended lazy-beds of potatoes.

Against this unchanging background eight years of a family's background may seem a small matter, yet, since records of human joys and sorrows are rare in the island's history, the chronicle may have its own value. It is a picture of life when the crofter-agitation of the late nineteenth century was dying down as hope of justice emerged from the Crofters' Commission and the Pentland Act, but when the great houses were still occupied by wealthy owners of deer-forests and salmon rivers. Armadale Castle was gradually falling out of occupation, but the white-painted steam-yachts still moved over the summer seas. Portree was a serious little community, inclined to brood on religious matters, so that the union of the U.F.s and the U.P.s was a slow affair, and the Free Presbyterians cast a shadow over mirth like rainclouds on the Cuillins. The Territorials in their scarlet coats and kilts of Cameron tartan marched to pipe and drum and drilled in Somerled Square, until the rainy morning in August 1914 when they sailed away on the *Gael* to be uniformed in khaki at Bedford, and to be cruelly cut down in the battle of Festubert.

So in this account of children growing up we have glimpses of Glenhinisdale and Braes; of a Raasay wedding in January rain and a Macleod wedding in late autumn sunshine; of the 1909 election and King Edward VII's memorial service, and warships in the bay; of epidemics and shortages, soirées and Communions; of daft Norman and the young doctor and the queerness of ministers and Lady Macdonald's sewing-party. And always in the background were the crofters whose tiny fields of oats or potatoes edged with corn marigolds and gated with old bed-heads covered every level part of the island. Ronald Macdonald came from this background, and during his shortened life he reconciled their affairs with the Congested Districts Board, especially on three occasions: when there was trouble at Elgol in 1908; after the Vatersay Raid in 1909 when crofters of Barra had seized and occupied land in defiance of the Board's allocations, and in 1910 when crofters of Idrigill near Uig in Skye tried to imitate their rebellion, and attacked the sheriff officer who came to serve evictions. In September of that year Lord Pentland, Secretary of State for Scotland and responsible for the Pentland Act came to confer with father about a just and reasonable settlement. The firm of Macdonald and Fraser supported the Board against the discontented crofters in these rebellions; only a recognised authority could help as many small-holders as possible, and it was the best hope of producing a redistribution of land by fair and legal means. Gradually during this period it was realised that the poor man's cause could be heard and judged with equity. There was no need to fight the Battle of Braes over again, or to suffer without redress the evictions and the rack-renting of a Major Fraser.